RETURN TO GLORY

Also by Matthew DeBord

Wine Country USA:
Touring, Tasting, and Buying at
America's Regional Wineries

The New York Book of Wine:
A City and Company Guide

RETURN TO GLORY

The Story of Ford's Revival and Victory at the Toughest Race in the World

Matthew DeBord

Atlantic Monthly Presss

New York

First Grove Atlantic hardcover edition: June 2017

Published simultaneously in Canada
Printed in the United States of America

FIRST EDITION

ISBN 978-0-8021-2650-4
eISBN 978-0-8021-8955-4

Library of Congress Cataloging-in-Publication data is available for this title.

Atlantic Monthly Press
an imprint of Grove Atlantic
154 West 14th Street
New York, NY 10011

Distributed by Publishers Group West

groveatlantic.com

17 18 19 20   10 9 8 7 6 5 4 3 2 1

For August, Mario James, and Dante
and for Detroit

Contents

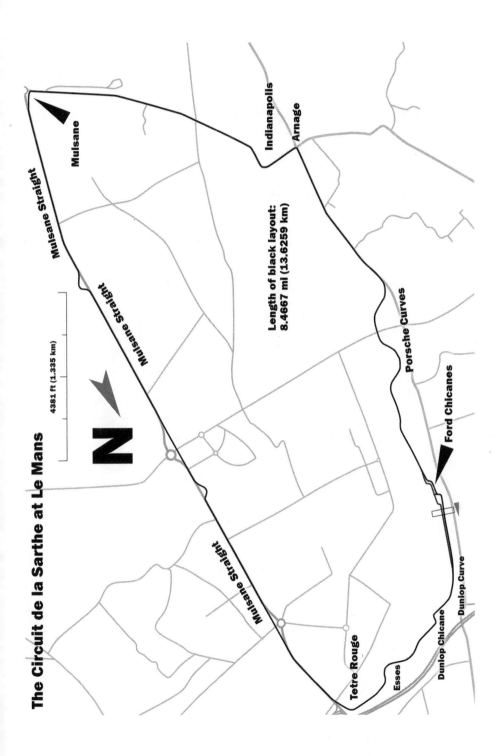

The Circuit de la Sarthe at Le Mans

Mulsane

Mulsane Straight

Indianapolis

Arnage

Length of black layout:
8.4667 ml (13.6259 km)

Porsche Curves

Mulsane Straight

4381 ft (1.335 km)

N

Ford Chicanes

Dunlop Curve

Dunlop Chicane

Esses

Tetre Rouge

Mulsane Straight

Prologue

June 19, 2016

It was morning in Le Mans, 130 miles southwest of Paris.

The preceding night had been pierced by the screams and howls of powerful race cars as they covered, endlessly it seemed, an eight-and-a-half-mile circuit first laid out in the early 1920s, when a race car was lucky to threaten 100 miles per hour. As French family dinners proceeded in tents and impromptu fireworks displays lit up the skies over the countryside, the engines' wails had continued. They'd raged on as bedraggled fans from all over the world grabbed a few hours of sleep in cars, campers, and tents strewn around grassy parking lots and fields.

In the cockpit of his Ford GT, the supercar Ford had built to commemorate its legendary win at the 1966 24 Hours of Le Mans—with, the plan was, a fresh win—Joey Hand had been pushing 200 miles per hour since sunrise. So far his average speed in the twin-turbocharged, 600-horsepower, low-slung race car was 150 miles per hour. He was sweating under his helmet, and inside his fireproof racing suit. He had shifted gears hundreds of times. He was thirsty, and he was getting tired.

The nighttime run hadn't worked out entirely in Ford's favor. There was a Ferrari in the mix. It was the number 82 car, a so-called privateer ride supported by Risi Competizione of Houston, Texas. Hand, a compulsively cheerful Californian in his mid-thirties, who had a taste for American flag–motif cowboy hats and McDonald's breakfasts—"I've won a lot of races with sausage Egg McMuffin in my stomach," he liked to say—was in the number 68 Ford GT, possibly the most anticipated high-performance machine in recent history. It had been designed from the ground up to win endurance races, Le Mans in particular.

The new GT had first "rolled a wheel," in racing parlance, fewer than 400 days earlier. There were now four GTs on the Circuit de la Sarthe at Le Mans, all red-white-and-blue and numbered 66, 67, 68, and 69—the years of Ford's Le Mans victories with the car's ancestor, the immortal GT40. And as the mid-morning snack lines formed outside the crêpe truck parked 100 yards from the pits, where the race cars pulled in for fuel and tire changes, Hand's GT was in second place.

One or another of the GTs had run in first place plenty during the event, which extended from the afternoon of June 18 to the afternoon of June 19—an entire solar day of racing, designed to break cars, to break drivers, and to break whole companies. When Ford had won this thing in epic fashion on the same weekend fifty years earlier, it had crushed Ferrari, the team that had dominated Le Mans from 1960 to 1965 with its seductive red track rockets fueled by the ego of Enzo Ferrari.

Now Hand was running down the latter-day version of those same red Ferraris Ford had beaten in '66. At the wheel of the Ferrari 488 GTE, a gorgeous twin-turbo, V-8–powered wedge of the finest Italian engineering and design, was Matteo Malucelli, a swashbuckling thirty-one-year-old from Forlì, near Bologna, who had survived a devastating crash two years earlier.

This was the GTE Pro class of the World Endurance Championship. This was the 24 Hours of Le Mans, perhaps the most famous race in the world and easily the toughest, a brutal test of driver and machine.

Hand and Malucelli were racing and racing hard.

The pouring rains that had beset the previous afternoon's start were long gone. With the sun rising in the sky, Hand sensed his moment. The setup was perfect. He was right on Malucelli's bumper—or, more accurately, his carbon-fiber diffuser, an aerodynamic component that extended low from the Ferrari's rear. Because Hand's car had been the fastest in qualifying, and fast enough to win the pole position, he knew he had the speed for a pass. He just had to pick his spot, find his moment—and not do something stupid, like overplay his chance and wreck the car.

He had Ferrari red in front of him, but a growling Ford Eco-Boost V-6 engine was behind him, pumping velocity to his rear wheels as violently as a fire hose pumping water. Hand had to hold his GT back just enough to have the extra punch when he needed it.

Malucelli wasn't on Hand's mind anymore. Hand had chased him for enough laps to gather the information he needed to do what he'd come to do, all the way from Sacramento, California, to this normally quiet but now raucous corner of France. Every year they hold this mad race and invite the best drivers and the finest cars in the world to destroy themselves—and the maddest part was coming up.

It's called the Mulsanne Straight—Les Hunaudières in French—a 3.7-mile stretch of tree-lined public road, where the fastest Le Mans racers, in the so-called prototype cars, can hit 250 miles per hour.

The Mulsanne Straight was the longest legal drag strip in the world, at least for this weekend. This was where Joey Hand was going to make his move. At 10:30 a.m., he peered through the eye port of his racing helmet and shifted in his racing suit. He remembered what Dave Pericak, the Ford executive heading up the Le Mans campaign, had said to him right before he got in the car: "Joey, go get 'em."

"That's the plan, boss," Hand had replied.

Hand checked the Ferrari in front of him. He gave the instruments one last scan. And then he went for it. Hand blasted the GT around the 488 and slipped in front of it, holding his position but preparing to defend it as he slowed from nearly 200 to 100 miles per hour to brake for the hard right turn at the end of the Mulsanne. From wherever they were watching, the thousands of Ford fans who'd descended on Le Mans rose to their feet. It was fifty years to the day since Ford had first won Le Mans, 113 years since Henry Ford started the company that still bears his name, and eight years since it had become apparent to everyone back at Ford headquarters in Dearborn, Michigan, that everything was going horribly wrong with the American auto industry.

Now, on a beautiful, clear morning in France, at one of motorsport's grandest venues, the spiritual home of Ford's greatest-ever racing victory, the carmaker's newest and most advanced piece of rolling technology was winning the 24 Hours of Le Mans. All anyone wanted to know at this moment was: *Will Ford be able to hold on?* Could history be repeated?

As the race continued, Joey Hand and his GT kept running at the front of the GTE Pro class. But the fact was, Hand had a Ferrari on his ass—a very fast Ferrari. And Ferrari drivers don't hold back, no matter where they race. They bleed *rosso corsa*, "racing red," the Italian national motorsports color. The red-white-and-blue of Hand's GT was putting a not exactly fine point on what this return to Le Mans was all about for Ford.

What's more, for Ferrari the race was personal. Ford had ended Ferrari's long Le Mans reign in the 1960s and after another three wins following the 1966 victory had backed away from Le Mans.

Ferrari never really came back, not with a full-on effort supported by the factory in Maranello. Instead, the car company that Enzo Ferrari had started at about the same time that Le Mans was born shifted its focus to Formula One.

In 2016, the Ferrari drivers and their teams didn't want to be accomplices to Ford's attempt to revisit that humiliating weekend, so long ago, yet so fresh. This was going to be a battle. This was going to be the most astonishing 24 Hours of Le Mans in decades. This was going to be Ford versus Ferrari, just like the good old days. It was a perfect story for racing fans, and it was now in its final chapter, just four hours before the checkered flag would drop.

At 10:31 a.m., Joey Hand was right where he wanted to be: *winning the race from the lead*. He wasn't hanging around behind the leaders, waiting to make a late pass. He was an American racing in a car bearing the name of the American who created the modern auto industry. He had twenty hours in the bank and four hours to go. This was going to be good.

It isn't often that one car completely dominates the conversation at a major international auto show. And it isn't often that one car so completely symbolizes a company's return from the brink of ruin. But that exact confluence happened in January 2015 in Detroit, at the North American International Auto Show, the biggest car show of them all.

The unveiling of Ford's new GT supercar was the culmination of a year of tantalizing rumors, which had begun to take shape in the fall of 2014 and then built momentum. The speculation went something like this: with 2016 right around the corner, the Ford Motor Company was seriously contemplating a return to what practically everyone in racing considers the automaker's moment of purest glory on the track, Le Mans in '66.

Everyone did the math: 2016 minus 1966 was fifty years. Ford had been through a lot in that half century. The company had always experienced ups and downs, of course. Although Henry Ford had pioneered the automobile, created the industrial production line, and even paid his workers a wage that enabled them to buy the cars that they were building, the company had been edged aside by General Motors before World War II. GM, the colossal model of the modern corporation, simply offered more choice.

But Ford had hardly been irrelevant in the years after that. It created beautiful sedans and produced what would become the best-selling vehicle in America for decades—the F-Series pickup truck. In the mid-1950s, the marvelous Thunderbird hit the road, defining in the process the sporty American coupe. In 1960, Ford introduced the Falcon, an innovative smaller car that stood in counterpoint to the massive cruisers of the Eisenhower era. The Escort, introduced in 1980, proved that the automaker could build a decent small car. The mid-1980s brought the Taurus, whose rounded shape would stand in contrast to the boxy sedans of the period; more than 7 million units would be sold.

Through the heyday of sport-utility vehicles in the 1990s and early 2000s, Ford's models sold well, starting with the Explorer, which has been in production since 1991. In the late 1990s, Ford's Lincoln division invented the luxury SUV market with the Navigator. The Mustang—the quintessential "faster horse" Henry Ford, quite possibly apocryphally, said was what his customers would have said they wanted, had he asked them—was and still is an American icon. Embedded in the national imagination, the Ford Mustang is celebrated in *A Faster Horse*, a well-received feature-length documentary that premiered at the 2015 Tribeca Film Festival.

And then there was racing. In this realm, Ford was less like an American car company than a European one. It proved its technology on the track and then put it in the cars it sold to the public.

The story of how Ford brought the GT40 to Le Mans in 1966 and went on to command the legendary endurance race is one of the most remarkable in the history of high-speed competition, not least for the business rivalry between Henry Ford II and Enzo Ferrari, which wound up being played out on the French racecourse. Since then the GT40 has been bound into Ford's DNA, for better or worse. To a certain extent Ford had been haunted by the GT40's success. You might even say cursed. Why, people wondered, has the storied American company never again been able to live up to that moment? With 2016 looming, the talk intensified: How could Ford *not* return to Le Mans for the fiftieth anniversary of the greatest victory of its greatest race car?

Destiny beckoned, it seemed, and by the late autumn of 2014 it was obvious Ford had something in the works. In the following January, at the Detroit auto show, the world saw what it was: a breathtaking conceptual expression of what a new GT would look like, in a street-legal version. It was a fearsome, futuristic carbon-fiber predator, painted a luminous blue, with an innovative six-cylinder engine mounted behind the driver. The overall design immediately put Ferrari, Lamborghini, Porsche, and a host of other exotic supercar manufacturers on notice.

That six-cylinder engine had something else going for it: a pair of turbochargers enabling—and this was what ultimately caused the collective dropping of jaws in Motown—600 horsepower.

Beauty was combined with power and set against a glorious racing backstory. As a stage setting, the GT introduction was masterly. But the vehicle also completely changed the conversation in the auto industry. Prior to the show, all anyone had been talking about was the arrival of self-driving cars—the latest chapter in the melding of the automobile and technology. With the debut of the

GT, speed was suddenly back in the picture, as was the prospect of actual human drivers—driving fast.

The city of Detroit and the Ford Motor Company were also back—although not without plenty of scars from the carnage of the financial crisis. Motown was smaller. The population had fled in droves, and the auto industry, once a symbol of American might, had dwindled in importance. The U.S. economy was now postindustrial, and Detroit, the definitive American industrial city, was learning to accept its downsized role. Once a proud Midwestern counterpoint to New York and Los Angeles, Detroit was a bankrupt shadow of its former self, with whole swaths of the metropolis given over to decay; some sections, remarkably, were even seeing the reclamation of the urban landscape by nature. In the winter of 2005, with the financial crisis looming, I'd been in the city for a meeting and staying at the hotel at GM's headquarters in the Renaissance Center downtown. At a late-evening dinner in the top-floor restaurant, looking out over the black Detroit River flowing with ice, I overhead a quartet of executives who'd also made the trip to Motown to talk to the biggest automaker in the United States.

"It used to be fun to come here," one of them said. The rest of the group nodded and mumbled in bleak agreement. Then they went back to their drinks.

Detroit had been to hell and back, as the now-classic 2011 Chrysler commercial starring the hometown rapper Eminem memorably drove home when it premiered at that year's Super Bowl. As had Ford. Prior to the 2008 financial crisis, the new Ford CEO, Alan Mulally, fresh off a successful stint at Boeing, stared into a bleak crystal ball and decided that Ford would run out of money in a few years—and in any case would struggle to weather even a normal downturn in the highly cyclical auto industry, let alone a massive international economic crisis.

So Mulally mortgaged literally everything Ford owned to the credit markets. It was a bold bet, but it paid off. When the crisis hit and the U.S. auto market collapsed, General Motors and Chrysler required bailouts and bankruptcy protection to survive. But Ford had Mulally's war chest.

Ford was a proud survivor. Within five years of that harrowing stretch, the company was healthy enough to start dreaming again. Against a backdrop of once-again booming U.S. auto sales and a balance sheet flush with cash, the Le Mans talk grew. Ford knew it had an opportunity to seize the kind of moment that might never come around again. And yet the new GT almost didn't happen.

The initial plan, intermittently discussed in the post-financial-crisis period, had been to return to Le Mans with a track-worthy Mustang. It took a major executive push, coming from the top of the company beginning in 2014, to green-light the thrilling new machine while simultaneously organizing and funding a racing operation on two continents.

Ford continued to bask in the afterglow of having survived the financial crisis and the meltdown of the U.S. auto industry without taking government bailout money or declaring bankruptcy, like General Motors and Chrysler. There is no more iconic American car company than Ford (and yes, part of that iconography includes Henry Ford's anti-Semitism, a bigotry embedded in the culture that he helped promote). For all practical purposes, Ford invented the automobile for the majority of Americans. And when the dark period of the financial crisis was over it pushed its brand forward in ways that had somehow become unimaginable for a demoralized U.S. auto industry.

The force doing the pushing was Mark Fields, Ford's CEO, who got the job after Mulally retired in 2014. When he accepted the big seat, Fields outlined a new vision for Ford as an advanced mobility company far more than a carmaker. His plan was to prevent

Ford from ever slipping back to the bleakness of the 2009 period, while simultaneously preparing the company to meet the challenges of the twenty-first century—challenges coming not from GM or Chrysler or Honda or Toyota or Ferrari, but from Tesla, Google, and Apple.

At the same time, Fields didn't neglect Ford's racing legacy. He came to Le Mans for the first time in 2015 to preside over the introduction of the new GT race car and to inaugurate Ford's Le Mans campaign. He was back in 2016, watching the race as Joey Hand made his move on Ferrari on Sunday morning.

Fields often said he wasn't a crusty "car guy," but he knew what winning on the track meant to the company. And he had working for him Ford family members who also knew.

"I think racing is something that has always been a part of our DNA," Henry Ford III told me in early 2016. Ford III is the great-great-grandson of Henry Ford and the grandnephew of Henry Ford II, the executive behind the GT40's Le Mans wins in the 1960s. Le Mans regulations require that the GT race car have a road-going equivalent, and Henry III had taken on the job of overseeing the marketing of that version to buyers in the general public after the race. His Ford Performance team would live and breathe Le Mans, on a breakneck schedule, for a year.

"One of the things we're trying to do with Ford Performance is really use racing as kind of a laboratory and a test bed for innovation," Ford said.

In 2016, Ford's comeback from the financial crisis and its aftermath was complete. Wall Street still hadn't come around, and Ford executives sometimes grumbled about the stock price. But they didn't complain about their customers. In 2015, a record 17.5 million new cars and trucks were sold in the United States, and a huge number of them were Fords—in particular Ford pickup trucks, including the F-150, which had been completely revamped to be lighter and get better fuel economy.

Ford was once again solidly the number-two automaker in the United States, behind GM. But Ford had a story brewing for 2016 that its Motown competitor was going to find tough to match. If Ford won again at Le Mans, it would be a win for everyone who had faith in the idea that Americans could build cars—great cars. Cars to remember, like the cars we remembered from the 1950s and 1960s.

For me, the story began in 2015 over a meal in New York City. It would end at a racetrack in France, where I stood with the sound of screaming engines in my ears like mechanical thunder. There was the flash of fast machines, and history thick in the air.

This is that story.

PART I

THIS COULD ALL GO AWAY

Chapter 1

Betting the Farm

Bill Collins, Ford's suave and effective communications man in New York, told me what would become my favorite anecdote about Alan Mulally. He shared it over steaks in 2015, a full six years after the company that had practically defined American industry for the first half of the twentieth century had been on the verge of collapse.

As we were waiting for our rib eyes to show up, Bill began talking about how bad things had been in 2008, when the financial crisis had just begun to destroy the economy. Back then nobody was thinking about a steak house lunch, especially in Detroit. Survival was the key. Apocalypse had come to Motown. GM was headed toward bankruptcy. Chrysler was headed toward bankruptcy and eventual acquisition by a savvy, swaggering, argumentative, sweater-wearing, chain-smoking Italian-Canadian named Sergio Marchionne, the CEO of Fiat. Credit, the lifeblood of the auto industry, was nonexistent in the United States at the time. Lehman Brothers was bankrupt, and the grim rumor was that Goldman Sachs was dangerously close to the same fate. The only thing standing between America and Great Depression 2.0 was a bearded, soft-spoken Princeton economist, Federal Reserve chairman Ben Bernanke. In the White House, the lame duck George

Bush was alternately bewildered and exhausted. (After leaving office, he would retire to Texas to paint odd portraits of his own feet in the bathtub.) On the campaign trail, Republican presidential candidate John McCain doomed his bid by claiming that the crashing economy was going along fine and by adding Sarah Palin, the factually freewheeling and devoutly self-promotional governor of Alaska, to his ticket.

On the Democratic side, Barack Obama was reaping the benefits of Hillary Clinton's Wall Street ties. At the beginning of the campaign, he had had nowhere to run but on her left flank. Fate created an opening there. The near collapse of the banking system enraged voters, and the senator from Illinois took the revolutionary rage of Occupy Wall Street and transformed it into an appealing message of hope, which was summarized by an iconic poster created by street artist Shepard Fairey.

Meanwhile, the hyperventilating pundits on CNBC, whose Wall Street cheerleading and CEO fealty had looked like smart career moves just six months earlier, were screaming, "Sell! Sell! Sell!" Jim Cramer, the loudest cheerleader of them all, is still living down his dramatic reversal of sensibility about the boundless virtues of an unfettered stock market.

Back in Detroit, as Bill Collins told it, there was blood in the streets. The U.S. auto industry had seen rough times before. GM had barely dodged the Great Depression of the 1930s, and in the late 1970s and early 1980s the government had bailed out Chrysler. The car business is cyclical, and everyone who works in or around the industry, from the oil-change guys to the executive suite, knows that the downturns follow the upswings with grim frequency. There's no way to prepare for them, either, other than to pile up cash on corporate balance sheets. The only viable strategy is to lay in a war chest with the full knowledge that the nature of the business will force you to spend *all of it* in order to remain in the game.

As the election neared, it already felt as if the auto industry was on the downside of a downturn, although it was hard to tell, because the yearly sales numbers looked pretty good, gas wasn't wildly expensive, and Americans were still buying big trucks and SUVs.

But at that point GM was struggling. It hadn't posted a profitable quarter in years, and the carmaker was hemorrhaging money every month to maintain its far-flung operations and keep up with its legacy pension and benefit obligations. The company was running on debt, was constantly low on cash, and was posting staggering quarterly losses. Cynical outsiders were calling for GM to file for bankruptcy protection, but the board and leadership knew they wouldn't be able to prove that the company was a "going concern."

At Ford, the contrast with the good times was stark. An impressive 17.3 million vehicles had been sold in 2000, when Ford had $24 billion in the bank, a "cash hoard," as the *New York Times* called it, "one of the largest of any company in the world." And although that number declined slightly in the years before the Great Recession, sales plunged to just over 10 million in 2009—a year after the company's stock price had plummeted to unimaginable lows. Detroit had seen bad. It had been battered by the Big Three's decades of declining market share and ferocious competition from Japan and Germany (free trade is a bitch). And in Detroit's case, serving the most competitive car market in the world had become daily combat. For much of the 1970s and '80s, Detroit had been losing battles. But by 2009, it was losing the war.

Alan Mulally, who had joined Ford in 2006 after a successful run at Boeing, could see defeat and surrender over the horizon: Ford was poised to lose a knee-buckling $12.7 *billion* that year, according to the consulting firm McKinsey & Company. At the time, it was reported that Ford was going to cease production at ten factories, creating in one desperate gesture a vast amount of unused manufacturing capacity and a virtual army of idled autoworkers.

Ford's losses represented a healthy chunk of the market capitalization of the entire company. The pressing question when Mulally moved into the big chair at Ford, at age sixty-one, was whether a plane guy could do cars—whether the guy who had leaped from success to success at a plane maker could concoct a turnaround at a carmaker. But that turned out to be entirely the wrong question. What we should have been wondering wasn't whether the plane guy could be a car guy. It was whether there would *be* any more American cars once the financial crisis had finished savaging the most symbolic of national industries.

By the time Bill Collins and I met up for that New York lunch, Mulally looked like a genius. Convinced as soon as he arrived in Dearborn and got a look at Ford's books that the automaker didn't have the balance sheet to endure a downturn, he mortgaged all of the Ford Motor Company's assets—factories, real estate, inventories, the whole shebang—for $25 billion. He called it, wryly, Ford's "home improvement loan." But that was classic Mulally, earnestly downplaying a big bet. Mulally favored tan trousers, blue blazers, and red sweater vests; he wasn't going to adopt a uniform of intimidation at Ford. He didn't change his wardrobe even when he headed to Congress in the throes of the crisis.

In his manner, Mulally resembled a man on his way to church. His expressions were uniformly placid and optimistic. He lacked anything even vaguely resembling rage. Steady beams of bright Midwesternness emanated from his eyes. If you met him at a bar, you would be surprised, because men like Alan Mulally don't go to bars. I watched him bound onto a stage in the years immediately following the financial crisis and half expected him to start singing campfire songs. The overwhelming impression Mulally delivered was deep trustworthiness. But it was entirely an act. Ford was his big chip, and he was all in.

When he mortgaged the farm, Mulally hadn't come across as a genius. He'd come across as desperate. At the 2007 Detroit auto show I had sat with some journalist colleagues and tried to draw a bead on what Mulally's Ford was all about. Apart from the pickup-truck business—the Ford F-Series has been the best-selling vehicle in America, year after year, since sometime before the start of the Vietnam War—and a certain iconic muscle car, there wasn't much to point to. "It's a pickup and Mustang company," I concluded, with a dismissiveness I would come to regret.

I didn't think Ford would be able to turn itself around—to re-invent itself, to abandon any of its old attitudes, or retain the no-longer-justified reputation for consistently achieving great things. It all just seemed like hubris. In Detroit, the men and women who run the American auto industry haven't yet discovered the false modesty that defines executives in newer business cultures. CEOs don't sit with the troops in open-plan offices, where status is erased by professional geography. The auto-industry big shots have big of-fices, with big views. If you're seeking the last gasp of the American mid-century style of business, Detroit is it. Everyone wears a suit, and the higher-ups often wear suits that are quite sharp. Very expen-sive Swiss watches are the rule. The smoking has largely vanished, but there's no shortage of drinking. The industry does business over beer, wine, and liquor—and doesn't apologize for it. I thought these guys didn't have a chance at another act. Ford and the rest of the carmakers were going to be done in by an excessive, inflexible pride in their past, and outpaced by the radical new business ideas of the Googles and Apples and Teslas, companies that didn't make things so much as create experiences—albeit cold, virtual ones.

Mulally wasn't exactly of that old auto-industry culture, coming from Boeing and its hard-core aerospace and defense-engineering culture, where they're always trying to think a few decades into the future. But he was the CEO of Ford, so he did his work in a big room.

Bill Collins described Mulally's office, a sizable affair on the twelfth floor of Ford's headquarters in Dearborn, a place known colloquially as the Glass House, in reference to its extensive use of the material. The office has a view of the legendary River Rouge plant that Henry Ford built over more than ten years, throwing open the doors in 1928. In its heyday, the Rouge was a factory where train cars full of iron ore rolled up at one end and finished cars rolled out at the other. Thunderbirds and Mustangs were built there. At one point the facility had its own river freighter, the SS *William Clay Ford*, named for Henry Ford's grandson. Vehicles are still built in the 600-acre facility, now called the Rouge Center. Alan Mulally got to look at it every day.

"Bill," Mulally said to Collins one day, as they sat in that office, "I look over there"—to the east and downtown Detroit—"and I can see GM."

Mulally paused. Collins waited.

"And if I look over there," Mulally gestured north toward Auburn Hills, thirty-five miles away. "I can just see Chrysler."

Detroit sits on a vast, flat plain in the Upper Midwest, on the banks of the Detroit River. If you're up high, you can see for miles. You can see Canada. And you can, if you're Alan Mulally, see the future.

"I do this all the time, because I like to keep an eye on everyone. But I also do it to remind myself of something," Mulally said. "I remind myself that this could all go away."

That was quite a black realization, it occurred to me as Bill finished the story, to be living in the mind, the conscience, of one of the country's most important industrial leaders at a time of crisis. Yet Mulally is a man who smiles easily. He is driven not by fear but rather by the optimism of someone who spent much of his career overseeing the design and construction of huge machines that can fly 600 miles per hour at 35,000 feet.

Ford, and the auto industry generally, brought Mulally back down to earth. The financial crisis and the Motown meltdown meant that the landing was anything but soft. It was a full-on crash. At one point, Ford's stock price fell to $1.24. The joke at the time was whether you "wanted fries with that." There was a certain amount of untoward celebration about not just Ford's struggles but also GM's and Chrysler's. At the extremes, some pundits argued that the government should simply let the industry go and allow it to rebuild itself through either traditional bankruptcy or liquidation. But that overlooked a pair of critical factors.

First, with credit locked up because of the banking crisis, there was no one *but* the government to provide bankruptcy financing. And even if financing had been available, an executive such as GM CEO Rick Wagoner knew from experience that a carmaker of GM's size wouldn't be able to sustain itself through a conventional Chapter 11 restructuring. GM's parts-making arm, Delphi, had been spun off in the decade before the financial crisis to satisfy Wall Street's desire to see GM unlock some trapped value. But Delphi had fallen into bankruptcy and languished in Chapter 11 for years, with GM providing the funding.

Second, it was unclear whether the solvent players in the U.S. industry—the transplants from Japan, Germany, and South Korea—would be able to take over Detroit's manufacturing capacity. The Big Three employed hundred of thousands of workers in dozens of plants, many assembling the trucks and SUVs that tended to satisfy the U.S. markets. Toyota and Honda built mainly cars at their U.S. plants. The Big Three also supported an extensive supply chain in the Midwest. Their financing arms generated billions in auto loans. As much as critics of the U.S.

industry—including those longtime detractors who continued to think that the Big Three built crappy cars and existed mainly to keep the United Auto Workers in business—might have fervently hoped to see a day of reckoning that would vaporize 100 years of industrial history, there were some very practical considerations in a market that *should* require at a minimum 14 million to 15 million new cars and trucks every year.

Everyone in the industry knew that the crisis, as bad as it had gotten, was not going to last forever. Barring complete economic collapse, an annual U.S. vehicle market of merely 10 million units simply wasn't conceivable. Beyond those core issues, there was also the national security question. Even if, say, Toyota, Honda, BMW, and Mercedes had been able step in, was it really advisable to turn over the most advanced and sophisticated industrial enterprise in the world to companies not based in the United States?

Ultimately, President Obama got behind the bailouts of GM and Chrysler and turned the challenge of saving Detroit over to "car czar" Steve Rattner, an erstwhile investment banker and Democratic political supporter who during the 2008 election had longed to become treasury secretary in a Hillary Clinton administration. In a 2010 *Vanity Fair* story about Rattner's ambition, William D. Cohan called his desire to lead Treasury "one of the biggest open secrets in New York's social and financial circles." Rattner's job was to deal with the Chapter 11 issues and Chrysler's bondholders, while a second member of the team, Ron Bloom, would tackle the UAW and its sprawling legacy costs. Another staffer would devote his full attention to GM.

There was no question that GM would be saved, but Chrysler was another story. It had already been bailed out once before. And the company had been kicked around and disastrously operated for a period by Daimler before being acquired by Cerberus

Capital Management, a private-equity firm. Cerberus couldn't do any better than Daimler, so by the time the crisis hit, Chrysler was a basket case. Obama and his advisors wanted to let it go, but the hangover of the Lehman catastrophe was still fresh. Fiat's Sergio Marchionne arrived with a plan to effectively take over the management of Chrysler, assuming the government's problems in exchange for its provision of the billions in financing that a rapidly executed bankruptcy of the automaker would demand.

Looking back, the hasty and controversial decision-making process that unfolded between the autumn of 2008 and the spring of 2009—with a presidential election thrown in—has been vindicated in its mostly improvisational wisdom. The more vehement critics of the bailouts and bankruptcies of GM and Chrysler, notably Mitt Romney (whose father had been an auto-industry executive before ascending to the governor's office in Michigan), were mistaken in their dogmatic attitudes toward unfettered capitalism and competition in the midst of a nearly unprecedented crisis. By the end of 2015, the U.S. auto industry had decisively recovered, setting a new record for annual new vehicle sales at the end of the year—17.5 million cars and trucks had rolled off dealer lots and into driveways and garages from sea to shining sea. GM, Chrysler (now Fiat Chrysler Automobiles), and Ford are now firmly re-ensconced as the Big Three. (Or at least the Detroit Big Two plus Fiat Chrysler.) But it had been a hell of a fight.

At GM, Mark Reuss, now CEO Mary Barra's right-hand man, performed a vital yet familiar role for the automaker: the car guy. Before him, this had been the job of Bob Lutz, an outspoken former U.S. Marine, who at one point flew fighter planes in his spare time but who had also worked in the European auto industry and, during a spell at Chrysler, had been a confidant of Lee Iacocca. Lutz was on the ground when GM CEO Wagoner was taking his fall. But Lutz survived and took on an ever more important position after the bailout and the bankruptcy. After Lutz left, and a series of CEOs passed the baton to Barra, Reuss answered the call.

Reuss may have been disappointed that he didn't get the top job—this has been widely discussed, rumored, and hashed over to the point that some felt he would bail on a lifetime at GM when the announcement was made. But he stuck around, and it was a good thing he did. He had the experience of having fought in the trenches to save the business.

Reuss would later turn out to be a central player in the rivalry between Ford and Chevrolet that was reignited by the GT's return to Le Mans, where it would face off against not just Ferrari but also Corvette Racing, a team that had been tearing it up in the GT Le Mans sports-car class in the years before 2016. Reuss, like Lutz, is a hell of a driver. Maybe not pro-racer level, but he holds the official qualifications that tell you he's not going to baby a 550-horsepower Vette or Caddy through a turn. He's going to drop the hammer.

Reuss does business the way he drives: on the edge, but with an inspiring degree of precision and expertise. In person, Reuss is that guy you wish had been your dad's best friend: cheerfully gruff, with a passion for what he does, but a straight shooter who tells it like it is. You want him as a boss for the inspiration—but you also know that you're going to have to live up to his expectations. He wears a tailored suit and wears it well, but he also has his own racing helmet.

"That time period was pretty surreal," Reuss told me, when I asked him about the crisis years. In the mid-2000s he was running Holden, GM's Australian division. Holden is where all the car guys want to wind up at some point. While the rest of the world, over the decades, has replaced old-school American rear-wheel-drive muscle with front-wheel-drive decorum or all-wheel-drive soccer-mom mobiles, and of course various varieties of hybrids, Holden operates in the land that time forgot. Aussies have a term for driving in an enthusiastic manner: *hooning*. And you don't hoon in a Toyota Camry. You hoon in a Holden Commodore, with a nice, big V-8 sending power to a pair of furiously spinning back wheels.

"At GM, we had a lot of different CEOs and leadership back then," Reuss said. After Wagoner departed, Frederick "Fritz" Henderson, who had been with GM since the first Reagan administration, took the job, in March 2009. He lasted less than a year. Then Ed Whitacre, a lanky Texan, who had run AT&T before joining the GM board, took over. In autumn of 2010 came Dan Akerson, who had joined GM's board from the Carlyle Group, a private-equity firm.

"There were a lot opinions about the company that were very public," Reuss recalled. "They were coming from people who were close to the TARP funds." TARP was the Troubled Asset Relief Program, the official name for the bailouts of GM and Chrysler, as well as the money that was pumped into the banking system during the financial crisis by the U.S. Treasury and the Federal Reserve: $425 billion in total, with roughly $80 billion going to the U.S. auto industry.

"You're totally defensive," Reuss added. "Everybody's got a pen. Everybody's got the Internet."

At GM, there was also the matter of the automaker's hidebound legacy. It was, for better or worse, the definitive hierarchical corporation, a bastion of bureaucracy, a citadel of Organization Man and Woman. A colleague once told me a great story about "old GM," the GM of the 1950s, '60s, '70s, and even '80s. He showed up for a meeting and was told to wait outside the conference room while some staffers attended to something.

"What are they doing in there?" he eventually asked.

"They're lining the room," was the reply.

"What's lining the room?"

In the conference room—one of those classic corporate spaces, with a huge fine-grained wooden table surrounded by chairs, the kind you routinely see in movies but rarely encounter in real life— a crew of GM employees had stretched taut lines of string in right angles across the table's expanse to precisely align leather business portfolios, pads, pens, and glasses. That was what the executives who were about to meet expected: rote precision.

The financial crisis didn't completely do away with this aspect of GM's culture—the place still runs on a rigorous timetable, and offices are typically manicured in a way that would baffle the average Silicon Valley tech worker who gallops between Ping-Pong table and espresso machine—but it did humanize a company that had woven together a bizarrely successful combination of industrial dominance, employee loyalty, and systematic dehumanization.

Reuss was part of the revolution. "The truth is that GM isn't a bunch of silos sitting on the Detroit riverfront," he said, in a reference to the Renaissance Center, the John Portman–designed complex distinguished by its five steel-glass-and-concrete towers, which serves as GM's world headquarters.

"GM is the people who build the cars," he said. "The company was talked about as some entity back then. But the company is people—and those people had incredible resilience. But in those days it was really hard. Everyone went home at the end of the day not knowing if they were going to have a job. That was pretty tough."

The restructuring was an ordeal, and from Reuss's point of view, it changed attitudes not just inside GM but also across the industry. He had the good fortune to be distanced from the often-unpleasant proceedings. Reuss's frontline seat for the Detroit meltdown wasn't in Detroit. It was a day's flight to the bottom of the world.

"On a daily basis, Holden was difficult, but it was also reward-ing," he said. Reuss and his team truly were off the grid, running the business on whatever cash came in the door that day, as their lines of credit vanished. Major global companies don't operate this way—credit is the lubricant that prevents them from seizing up.

But the financial crisis changed all that. Even General Electric lost access to the credit markets, leading Jeff Immelt to call Henry Paulson, the treasury secretary at the time, in a baffled panic about GE's inability to issue short-term debt. No key business leader had ever worked this way.

In Australia, Reuss had few choices. It was do or die.

"You could see it start to work," he recalled. "It was an amazing time. We were making it happen, but it was hand to mouth—everything or nothing."

Then he said something everyone in business dreams of saying: "We were able to create our own destiny."

If you do get to create your own destiny, Reuss now contends, you can't be seduced by success into taking it for granted.

"We haven't allowed ourselves to be satisfied," he insisted, when I asked him whether he ever goes home after a long day and allows himself a moment of back patting. "The business is extraordinarily difficult. And the only way to be successful is to not sit around and think about how great everything is going. The enjoyment I feel in the job is not sitting back and reflecting."

That said, he does allow himself the odd moment of joy when he takes in the racing performance that GM has turned in. " 'Take no prisoners' and 'Never give up'—those are the two mottoes Chevy racing and GM live by."

While Reuss was digging around in his office sofa for loose change Down Under, waiting for a chance to get back to the track to watch Corvettes win trophies, Mulally had his hands full over at Ford. He had to put the carmaker's finances on the line, rally the troops and his executive leadership, assuage the concerns of a vast network of dealers, retool the company's unwieldy collection of brands, resist the urge to focus exclusively on the United States while the business in Europe and China was also under incredible stress, and keep track of the agony that Detroit itself was going through (the city would lurch into bankruptcy in July 2013).

It almost goes without saying, but through this wrenching process, a return to endurance racing and to the legendary turns and straightaways of Le Mans was a million miles away from Mulally's thinking. If he couldn't save the company that was building Ford F-150 pickups and Mustangs for America, he was never going to be able to get behind a new GT and a reconquest at Le Mans.

When Mulally had arrived at Ford, he discovered a mess. Actually, it was more than a mess—it was a looming catastrophe. The reign of Jacques Nasser as CEO from 1999 to 2001 had demoralized the company and saddled it with a cacophony of brands and models ranging from the posh Jaguar to base versions of the F-150 pickup that were intended to ferry bales of hay around ranches. After Nasser, William Clay Ford Jr. had taken over the family business. Bill is another of Henry Ford's great-great-grandsons, but as well intentioned as he was, he lacked the skills to run a twenty-first-century global manufacturing company. By the end, his job was to stave off bankruptcy, an imperative driven by the entrenched resistance of the Ford heirs to seeing their incomes threatened as the value of the assets they held was laid low. A merger would have made sense, but nobody wanted to merge. And at this time, the high-flying car company executives who could execute were also prima donnas of the highest order. An effort to woo Renault-Nissan's rock-star chief executive Carlos Ghosn was met head-on by Ghosn's titanic ego and his desire to be the one man at the top of the Ford hierarchy.

Actually, Ghosn's instinct made sense. Like all legacy automakers, Ford had evolved to a point at which working for Ford, not building and selling quality cars, seemed to be the first priority for many execs. In the industry, this problem has always been most evident at GM, where the divisional structure effectively separated the car making from the mother ship. GM's executive suite oversaw a financial enterprise that was also an insurance company, for all practical purposes, looking after obligations to retirees that had been negotiated in more flush times. This left the heads of the divisions free to make their own luck, by whatever means necessary. And why not? Running Chevrolet or Buick was like having your own car company to play with. The autonomy was a double-edged blade: GM got aggressive market competitors but at the cost of ferocious internal conflict for resources.

Ford's simpler structure avoided this classic GM problem. But of course Ford served the Ford family. Ford also had its own internal snarling and backbiting. That was the auto-industry way.

Mulally's personality and experience at Boeing brought a critical new element to the party: proactive teamwork and preemptive quality control. Mulally had overseen the development of the Boeing 777, one of the most successful aircrafts the plane maker had ever built and a critical successor to the legendary 747 jumbo jet. The 777 was a product of innovative collaboration, and since its wildly successful introduction in the 1990s, its development has become a widely used case study in business schools for its willful obliteration of the old "siloed" approach to manufacturing, in which functional groups worked independently, guarding their expertise until it came time to fight for resources—at which point the quality of the product was invariably degraded.

In the American car business, it was the task of marketers and ad agencies to cleverly—at times very cleverly—paper over the flaws with something snappy that spoke to brand enthusiasts. That doesn't work in the aviation industry, because the biggest advertisement for a Boeing is airlines ordering its planes and being satisfied with their performance. You don't spend some $200 million on a 777 because TV spots gush over the stitched leather seats or the quietness of the cockpit. The big jet has to speak for itself—and be able to do so over several decades of its service life with an airline.

With Ford's balance sheet shored up by the $25 billion credit line, Mulally could turn his attention to transferring the level of commitment he was familiar with from the aviation business to the auto business. You don't build bad planes, and you shouldn't build bad cars. But Mulally also had to remake Ford's culture at a time when that culture was in crisis.

What Mulally came up with was epic in its simplicity. He would promulgate a core message and make it his highest priority to ensure that every single employee of the Ford Motor Company understood and supported it.

No one had ever really done this before, not on such a scale, in the teeth of an existential crisis. Sure, there was the vaunted "Toyota Way," based on the principle of *kaizen*, or "continuous improvement." But *kaizen* wasn't a rallying cry; it was designed to intentionally undermine the ultratraditional Japanese deference to authority and empower all Toyota workers to contribute to making better cars. What Mulally wanted to do, in a sense, was revive a reverence for authority at Ford—but not a reverence for Henry Ford or the Ford family. Rather, he sought to convince employees that Ford was a brand they could pledge allegiance to in a way that bordered on the reverential. Again, this was the dark side of Mulally's personality turned to the work of the light: the gambler in the red Ford-logo sweater vest was also a cunning con man, and con men traffic in belief. What Ford needed more than anything else in the days before the financial crisis hit was something to believe in.

And so did Detroit.

★   ★   ★

In the twentieth century, Detroit brought prosperity to tens of thousands of blue- and white-collar workers. It occupied a special place in the national psyche. But eventually Americans began to see Detroit as a failed metropolis, one beset with social unrest and riots in the 1960s and malaise in the 1970s. And in the 1980s, when competition from Japan destroyed the Big Three's lock on the U.S. auto market, the city evoked the particular mixture of sadness and irritation that comes with faded glory.

Some of the distaste for the city that grew in the second half of the twentieth century is firmly rooted in certain cultural shifts, including demographic changes such as "white flight" from urban centers like the city of Detroit, where poor African-Americans remained, frustrated by entrenched economic and political inequality. Then there was the preoccupation with the rising "service economy" that took shape in the 1970s and 1980s. The future, apparently, belonged to the educated professionals who could organize and control complicated technologies and systems. But Detroit's is a tale of building stuff. It's not about managing the global flows of capital or creating media empires—those are New York's specialties. It's not comparable to the model that made Silicon Valley rise—which you might call the relabeling of computer science as computer engineering. It's not akin to Hollywood's creation and exporting of mega-mass-market entertainment.

Detroit lacks twenty-first-century sex appeal. And yet, as Detroit declined, Americans sensed that something essential was being lost. The city's problems were complex, culminating in its 2013 bankruptcy, the largest in U.S. history. But Detroit's attitude was always simple. What it did, in its view of itself, was make cars. And by making cars, the city and its surrounding towns made other things, most critically the American middle class. Unionized autoworkers made good money, even if Detroit didn't always build the most coveted cars. Auto executives had lived enviable suburban country-club lifestyles, but they weren't as wildly rich as their counterparts on Wall Street or in Hollywood (and later Silicon Valley). The Ford exec with the nice office in Dearborn felt an affinity with the guy who performed shift labor at an assembly plant building pickup trucks. In the most meaningful sense, they shared a dream, and to this day the people in the offices that steer the Big Three treat a plant visit the way New York gallery owners do a trip to an artist's studio, or a record executive does the studio session of an important band. They know this is where the magic happens.

But the magic doesn't have the same economic power it once did. The United Automobiles Workers union has witnessed its membership fade, while all around it organized labor in America has collapsed. But there are still the cars and what they symbolize: freedom, of course, but also the pinnacle of a certain type of American economic empowerment and a sharing of the wealth between management and labor. They continue to be a powerful rebuke to lazy Marxist thinking about the inevitable exploitation of labor, given that the immense labor force the auto industry created in the Upper Midwest was indeed a *force*, for social and political change.

In the other citadels of American power, the auto industry is borderline despised, and it is misunderstood or underestimated for precisely this reason. In Washington, the Republican right and even chunks of the Democratic left resent the power organized labor wields over politicians in Michigan and Ohio. In New York, Wall Street is baffled by the core proposition of the industry, which can create high-wage jobs at a clip that would stagger even the most avid libertarian technology entrepreneur. The fact that the automakers can operate as their own banks, using their profits to generate auto loans, doesn't enhance this relationship. (And the fact that they can't operate *fully* as banks, taking customer deposits, can exaggerate the differences, as it did during the financial crisis, when automaker finance companies couldn't obtain the funds they needed to make loans.)

In the United States, the automakers are also fortress employers, with a workforce that is assured of relative stability through the cyclical downturns that are a fact of its history. This obviously isn't the case in nonunion Detroit South—the southern U.S. auto-manufacturing states such as Tennessee, South Carolina, and Alabama—where workers are employed "at will" and can be laid off at any time. (Union workers are also laid off, particularly when plants are idled to adjust production, but the layoffs are often temporary, and the workers are hired back.)

The auto industry's economic power hasn't helped it remain relevant in the national economic narrative, however. While Motown was down in 2009 and climbing back from 2010 to 2013, Silicon Valley was riding high, at the height of its self-confidence (and, arguably, its arrogance) following its own meltdown when the dot-com bubble burst in the early 2000s. Apple was on its way to becoming the most valuable company in the world, displacing ExxonMobil. Google stock was trading in the thousands per share. Facebook's initial public offering heralded the arrival of a new kind of Web 2.0 technology company, one built of user-generated shared content rather than computers and devices (as Apple was) or packaged software (Microsoft).

Then there was Tesla, whose survival spurred a belief among major tech firms and start-ups alike that the landscape of mobility could be remade for a digital future. After an initial period of wariness, the carmakers were happy to partner with these schemes, bringing much more advanced technology into their cars.

Ford led the way, as Mulally delivered frequent annual keynotes at the Consumer Electronics Show in Las Vegas, enabling the CES to commence the process of displacing in importance some major car shows (mainly those of Los Angeles and New York). Later, Mark Fields intensified Ford's aggressive efforts to transform itself from a car company into a mobility company, as he often called it.

It was better to join Silicon Valley than to try to beat it. That was the prevailing wisdom, and it was understandable. During the financial crisis, the American automobile was seen as a problem to be solved by the Silicon Valley elites, who often drove luxury vehicles but lamented the state of information technology inside cars and trucks. Larger-scale issues also gripped them: the economic inefficiency of the automobile, pollution caused by the internal-combustion engines, and the relatively slow pace of innovation compared with that in consumer electronics and software.

A certain triumphalism also affected their attitudes, perhaps spurred on by their admiration for Elon Musk and Tesla (formerly Tesla Motors). Detroit had had its time in the American economic sun, but the iconic industry of the second industrial revolution was so twentieth century. The baton was being passed. Geeks writing computer code had won, while the gasoline-soaked engineers and slick executives of Detroit had lost.

Detroit auto executives also knew that their vehicles' development cycles wouldn't allow them to keep pace with rapid changes in consumer preferences for connected experiences. So they formed partnerships with Microsoft, Apple, and Google and began to cede control of the dashboard. By 2016, nearly every vehicle in GM's fleet would offer both Apple CarPlay and Android Auto as infotainment options, and the carmaker would install high-speed Wi-Fi connectivity across the board.

You could say that the Detroit automakers both sold out to Silicon Valley and ran up the white flag of surrender. You don't try to beat back a tsunami. By 2016, the Big Three were selling more cars than ever before, raking in the cash, and making sure

Silicon Valley had access to these rolling "platforms." Detroit was also designing and building its own self-driving cars and keeping pace with Tesla on the electric-vehicle front. This auto industry was confident. And at Ford, the company had its own visionary to thank for it—Alan Mulally, who looked out his Motown office windows every day not to bask in the trappings of his rise to the top but to remind himself that it could all disappear at any moment.

Chapter 2 ═══════

One Ford

If you want to get any current or former Ford employees to recall their finest hour, just ask them about "One Ford."

It's exceptionally uncommon for large global corporations, especially companies that are as competitive and internally territorial as those in the auto industry, to get all their workers on the same page.

General Motors has often been criticized as the American car company with the most political corporate culture and the most entitled attitude. But Ford has never been immune to internal strife or a healthy whiff of its own arrogance. In fact, Ford's strife was just as intense as its crosstown rival's, but it was of a different flavor. If GM was the defining example of the postwar American corporation—the organization chart as business destiny, according to its architect, former GM president Alfred Sloan—then Ford was the prime mover of the U.S. auto industry, and the ultimate family business. In the early twenty-first century, GM had no representatives of its founders, the men who created Cadillac and Buick, Oldsmobile and Chevrolet. But at Ford, members of the founding family still depended on the company for their livelihoods, either as idle heirs or as active participants in the business.

That Ford as a company was both the direct Ford family and the extended "family" of Ford employees, white collar and blue, was a strength and a weakness. On the one hand, being part of either family came with the opportunity to feel you were part of something larger than yourself. On the other hand, all families are dysfunctional in their own ways, and the Fords and their workers had had decades to refine that dysfunction.

In the years before the financial crisis, the sharp-elbowed rivalries and brutal internal politics inside Ford had created a culture that wasn't just afraid of change—it was antithetical to it. The atmosphere wasn't uniformly horrible, but being at Ford, whether in the executive suite or on a factory floor, and thinking of yourself as part of a greater mission was pointless. Job one, to borrow a phrase that has taken on legendary significance at Ford, was to protect your own ass. Once that was accomplished, you could protect the asses of those you needed for your advancement. A distant third priority was the naive notion that you should be wholly focused on building better cars and trucks.

But this is one thing you need to learn to appreciate, in every sense of that word, about the good and bad of the U.S. auto industry. A hundred years of building things with wheels and engines means that although its cars and trucks might not always resonate with the public—in fact, the public may vilify them—Detroit still *understands* the automobile. This understanding goes to some deep level where origin stories are wound into a glowing matrix of molten steel, burning rubber, an affluent postwar middle class, men in good suits overseeing it all, and the design and engineering of the machine that changed the world forever.

Detroit can freely draw on that, for the good of us all. As for the bad . . . well, at Ford, the core principle of the company as the vision of a determined entrepreneur and family man had been twisted into unrecognizable shapes.

Everything had gotten too slick, too careerist, too far from the legacy vision of "Fordism," which although severely tainted by Henry Ford's anti-Semitism and hard-core opposition to organized labor, nevertheless gave birth to the signature industry of the twentieth century and marked the high point in the ascent of industrial capitalism. Mass production of the automobile—the birth of transportation for everyone, to practically anywhere—was a very big idea. But at Ford, the legacy of that idea had led to its degradation; the game in the 2000s was to position yourself to thrive when business was good and to stock enough ammunition and canned goods to ride out the downturn and come out with your head still firmly attached to your body.

Alan Mulally changed all that. He called his plan One Ford, and it was transformational in its simplicity.

"At the heart of our culture is the One Ford plan, which is essentially our vision for the organization and its mission," he told McKinsey & Company's Rik Kirkland, senior managing editor of the consulting firm's publishing program, in an interview in 2013, long after the storm had passed and the plan had been vindicated.

"People here really are committed to the enterprise and to each other," he added. "They are working for more than themselves."

Mulally wasn't going to tolerate dissent. You were either on the bus or off the bus. "Some prefer to work in a different way," he told Kirkland. "Ultimately, they will either adopt the Ford culture, or they will leave."

When he came to the company, Mulally understood the stakes, which were stark. Ford wasn't just failing—it had been serially traumatized by Nasser's disastrous tenure and Bill Ford's well-intentioned but ineffective leadership. Mulally also understood that he could lead Ford's workers to sand and tell them it was water, and they would drink it because there was no choice. His leadership wasn't just inspired. It bordered on cultish.

But it worked. "It made one plus one equal three," as Mark Fields likes to put it. "It allowed us to rationalize everything globally," he adds.

It's worth noting that as we look back on the spectacular job Mulally did saving Ford, we should recognize that his innovations were largely managerial and leadership-oriented. His ideas about the products Ford should be building and selling were misguided. This was where the plane guy proved that although he could reform the car guys, he couldn't assess the marketplace as they did.

Of course, numerous industry outsiders shared his viewpoint. The book on Detroit was that it was getting passed by more innovative foreign automakers, many of which were building their cars and trucks in the United States, to be as close as possible to this critical market.

Mulally had read the book. He wanted Ford to press for more hybrids and fuel-efficient small cars, an understandable urge given that fuel efficiency had become a driving force in aviation. The Boeing airliners that Mulally oversaw made it an absolute priority. When he was doing the pressing, there was widespread analysis and punditry around the auto industry arguing that higher gas prices in the United States were a historic inevitability. "Peak oil" was much discussed—the theory that all the easily accessed oil on the planet had been discovered and that the great reserves of the Middle East were entering a time of declining productivity. A booming China, with a middle class that wanted nothing more than to own cars, was going to force oil-thirsty America to compete for a limited supply, driving prices to well above four dollars a gallon in the short term and probably toward European levels—ten, twelve, fifteen bucks a gallon—in a decade. On top of that, the U.S. government was raising its Corporate Average

Fuel Economy, or CAFE, standards, demanding that automakers hit much higher combined MPG (miles per gallon) ratings across their fleets.

It was all wrong. And it was all wrong at high levels. In Steven Rattner's book about the crisis, *Overhaul: An Insider's Account of the Obama Administration's Emergency Rescue of the Auto Industry,* President Obama is reported to have asked why Detroit couldn't build a Corolla, the popular compact sedan from Toyota. The problem with that question is that it represents, in a lofty nutshell, why a lot of people, some of them extremely powerful, don't get Detroit. They're easily distracted by trends on the East and West Coasts and by the grand visions of futuristic disrupters of the status quo. Everyone has told them for decades that the Japanese make a superior car. It has become received wisdom.

But it overlooks two things. First, small cars don't sell for much, so the profit margin on them is modest. You have to manufacture a lot of them for not much payoff—or any payoff at all. Detroit *could* build a Corolla, millions of them, but it had no real incentive to do so over the long haul, and certainly no justification for making such a car the center of a portfolio of vehicles.

Second, there's the simple fact that the U.S. auto market is enormous and made up of numerous segments. In America, you never have the experience of looking out across a highway and seeing a sea of hatchbacks, with the occasional small delivery van tossed in, as I did when I traveled to France in June 2016 for Le Mans. In France, and for that matter much of Europe, there is one car segment, and it is compact gas sippers that don't cost much and can traverse the tight roads of the continent's ancient cities.

In America, no one segment ever rules the road. The industry is cyclical, not just in overall sales, which can rise and fall by several million per year; it's also cyclical in demand for large trucks and SUVs and for smaller vehicles. In 2009 and 2010, when gas prices spiked in much of the country, sales of gas-electric hybrids and compact cars rose, as truck and SUV sales declined. But starting in 2013 and 2014, pickup and SUV sales roared back. That meant substantial profits for the Detroit truck makers (the Japanese and Germans also did OK with their SUVs). All these trends are relative, of course. Total pickup sales are always higher than those of other vehicles in the United States, but automakers depend on selling lots of them year after year.

Basically, the U.S. auto market is driven by employment and gas prices. In America, if you have a job and gas is cheap, you will be more likely to buy a big truck (whether it's an Escalade or an F-150 will depend on your level of affluence). Whenever these conditions hold, Detroit will enjoy a happy time. When they don't hold, Detroit will suffer.

After all the dire talk about a permanent shift to higher gas prices, in 2015 and 2016, the price of oil collapsed; fracking for oil in once-inaccessible regions of the United States helped contribute to a worldwide glut in crude oil. Supply rapidly outpaced demand—remember, the number of miles that Americans were driving annually had been reduced by the financial crisis—and the familiar economic law took hold. In suburban New Jersey, I could buy gas for less than two bucks a gallon. It reminded me of when I first moved to Los Angeles in 2004 and could purchase California's specially formulated gasoline (always pricier than gas anywhere else in the country) for just $1.25 a gallon. By the time we left in 2014, however, it had been costing us seventy-five dollars or more to fill up our Honda Odyssey minivan in the Golden State. I was flatly astonished the first time I pulled up to a pump in the Garden State. I readied a pair of twenties, but by the time I had filled up on regular, I owed eighteen dollars. OK, sure, I was filling up a Toyota Prius, but it was still a shock to realize how far gas prices had tumbled back down.

With gas cheap, Ford was raking it in—but not because the company was selling small cars and hybrids. The SUV market had roared back, as Americans had happily returned to their old ways. The bottom line is that in America, for the most part, we don't drive small cars. Or, more accurately, we will *sometimes* drive small cars, but only if there are extreme spikes in the price of gas, for instance in the 1970s or the late 2000s.

Ford had loads of SUVs and a new type of car-based utility vehicle called a crossover to sell, plus the F-150. It was these vehicles, not the futuristic cars of tomorrow, that bolstered Ford's post-crisis bank account, as the U.S. auto market surged toward the 2015 sales record of 17.5 million new cars and trucks. Meanwhile, China became a 20-million-per-year market, and the Chinese were becoming as addicted to SUVs as Americans.

So, there were the actual vehicles that Ford was selling, and there was the new corporate philosophy that Mulally had introduced. Fortunately, they were mutually supportive, even if the SUVs didn't fit with Ford's crisis-era attitudes about the types of cars and trucks that were going to define the recovery. (In retrospect, Detroit was lucky that the SUVs had staged a comeback, as the return to large-and-in-charge also meant much juicier profits, helping to more rapidly bolster Ford's bottom line and to enable the carmaker to add tens of billions in cash to its balance sheet.)

"One Ford" was such a simple message that Mulally could fit it on a single card, which he printed in quantity and handed out. When I first heard about it, it reminded me of the famous "business plan" that tech giant Intel created in 1968. Cofounders Robert Noyce and Gordon Moore needed to raise capital for their idea, which effectively was to leave Fairchild Semiconductor, a company that for all practical purposes nurtured Silicon Valley. Noyce and Moore were working with some early venture capitalists and were asked to outline what they planned to do.

The outline they created was all of three paragraphs, typos and all. "The company will engage in research, development, and manufacture and sales of integrated electronic structures to fulfill needs of electronic systems manufacturers," was the pitch. It got the Intel cofounders $2.5 million, for a company that now has a $100 billion market cap.

Engineers are always seeking the simplest solutions to problems, and like Noyce and Moore, Mulally was an engineer. So he crafted the One Ford plan as four key objectives, easy to understand, easy to memorize, easy to repeat to anyone who asked:

1. Bring all Ford employees together as a global team.
2. Leverage Ford's unique automotive knowledge and assets.
3. Build cars and trucks that people want and value.
4. Arrange the significant financing necessary to pay for it all.

It isn't difficult to grasp both the vision that Mulally was striving to outline and the considerable challenges that One Ford faced. Ford employees weren't a global team—they were disorganized and "siloed," to use the business-school term for groups of workers and managers who are trapped in their own subworlds of the larger business. Additionally, teamwork wasn't prioritized; individual competition and survival were.

Ford was in retreat, like the rest of the auto industry, and fighting the widespread assumption that its technology was of the twentieth century, not the twenty-first. But Mulally knew that auto design, engineering, and manufacturing were technologically sophisticated—much harder undertakings, in many ways, than creating software companies. At a fundamental level, even an inexpensive car needs to be able to withstand rigorous crash testing. Automobiles are made up of thousands of parts, and many of them have to be constructed with great precision. Components have to last for more than a few years. Auto plants are full of huge, multimillion-dollar robots that can sling around an entire chassis while still applying exacting welds. Car designers and engineers now use the latest computer technology to imagine and execute vehicles, and the industry has in recent years been on a hiring spree for computer scientists, as the brains of cars and trucks become increasingly sophisticated—and vulnerable to hackers.

So the car business aims for innovation, but not at the same paranoid and frantic pace as Silicon Valley. Over the course of more than a century, the various technologies that go into the automobile have been refined, re-refined, and extensively fine-tuned. The car that you drive today, one that costs less than $20,000 new and may run for over a decade, resides at the peak of 100 years of industrial evolution.

It says something about the "traditional" auto industry's appetite for change that Tesla is the first company to come along with a completely different idea since the internal-combustion engine asserted its dominance prior to World War I. Tesla's innovation is not about cars—Tesla's vehicles don't look radically different from what's already on the road—but about how cars should be powered. Automakers had experimented with electric cars before Tesla's arrival—both GM and Toyota sold or leased them in the 1990s, in small numbers—but no one had ever made a 100 percent commitment to going electric.

Just because an automaker like Ford is very good at building millions of cars annually doesn't mean the extravagant cost of doing the building has been substantially reduced since the 1950s. In some respects, it has gone up, as consumers have demanded (and the government has required) ever more safety and technology features. Some companies blow through money. Automakers positively inhale it in massive quantities. A billion bucks is nothing to a big global carmaker. That's about the basic cost to develop a new version of the Ford Focus or Explorer. Designers, engineers, accountants, computer scientists—none of them come particularly cheap, and it takes hundreds and hundreds of people to design those cars, let alone manufacture, market, and sell them. Under normal, non-recessionary conditions, this is fine. So much money sloshes through Ford's, GM's, or VW's accounts and various lines of business that the capital-intensive nature of the business is manageable. But when the downturns come, as they always do, a car company's mettle is tested.

Mulally had taken care of the capital challenge with his home-improvement loan. But in his mind that was just the beginning. Ford wasn't capitalizing on its uniqueness.

Point three of Mulally's plan was a bit dicey. Mulally thought Ford had lost touch with the market—and to a degree it had. But in some areas, particularly trucks and SUVs, the market had just temporarily shifted away from Ford owing to external economic pressures. Nonetheless, Ford could be better prepared for these shifts.

One Ford would of course fail without the billions needed to pull it off. To my mind, this is the most poorly understood aspect of Mulally's plan: even a simple strategy can cost a lot to execute. One Ford is now a business-school case study, frequently reviewed and pondered by academics. It has also achieved the status of a folk legend. I've met Ford employees who still have their tattered One Ford cards, which they carry with them everywhere. When I describe the One Ford plan now, I always note that I've never seen such unity in a business before. *No one* at Ford failed to get it.

But as simple as the One Ford plan was, its success relied on an enormous infusion of cash: $25 billion (in contrast to Noyce and Moore's $2.5 million). This is important. You don't transform major companies on the cheap. Real change required real investment. Without those billions in the bank, it ultimately wouldn't have worked.

In the twenty-first century, with Internet companies such as Instagram and WhatsApp being bought for billions after a few years of work, with staffs in the low double digits, there's a general and pernicious assumption among putative new-business experts that the way to go is cheap and fast—the vaunted "lean start-up." But that isn't always the case. Chrysler, GM, and Ford—along with the U.S. network of auto suppliers and auto dealers—account for around 5 percent of the U.S. economy. Fixing something that big can't be done on a budget.

Although it can be done fast, as Mulally discovered. When he took the CEO job in 2006, it was apparent that he needed to work with urgency, but the financial crisis accelerated that imperative. It wasn't a turnaround that he faced—it was survival.

Mulally didn't radically revamp the management team, although some executives did eventually depart. Rather, he pressed his managers to collaborate. For some, this was unthinkable: they were Ford lifers who had honed their skills in the old arena, where job one was to take care of number one.

But circumstances dragged an impressive number of them along with Mulally on his journey, a fortunate development, as the new CEO didn't have time to remake the company's leadership. But he had to convince the executives who would commit to his One Ford vision that it was essential to learn two critical new lessons: First, information had to be shared across the company—information both good and bad. Second, to put it bluntly but truthfully, though in words that Mulally would never use, it was OK to fuck up.

The traditionally male-dominated auto industry is a profane place. You have to get used to highly successful businessmen in beautiful suits, men from the United States and Europe, throwing around language that would make a marine blush. There are now many more women in the business than there were in the past, and they're tough as well, never hesitating to trot out the rough language when they need to.

But saying that something is fucked up, as people in the car business became used to doing, and actually admitting you're the one responsible for fucking something up are two completely different things. The former is an assessment, while the latter is a confession. And asking for forgiveness in the auto industry has typically been regarded as a one-way ticket to the unemployment line.

At Ford, the culture had evolved not so much to mask fuckups but rather to avoid confronting them until it was too late. Then you could shrug your shoulders, enact your carefully cultivated blame-somebody-else strategy, and challenge the company to pony up for a fix or simply kick the problem down the road. Ford wasn't alone in this, of course. It was the entire U.S. car business. The culture was nothing like that of a Japanese automaker, where failure could lead to a ritual admission of responsibility and an apology, a cleansing process. In Detroit, the toxic avoidance piled up.

Mulally didn't want a whole bunch of fragmented Fords where failure was punished. He wanted one Ford where failure was embraced either as a learning process or as an early trigger to devote team resources to salvaging a product. I thought of it as similar to the way that a healthy body fights off an infection: hitting red alert and swarming the invading bacteria or virus with immune defenses, and thereby temporarily weakening the body's tendency to have its various parts and systems focused on their own businesses, so that the sickness could be eradicated. This was short-term unpleasant but long-term advantageous. Under Mulally, if there was trouble, a bright light was shone on it, and the resources to alleviate it were mustered. Problems weren't owned by single managers; in the pre-Mulally era, that single ownership had functioned as a sort of perverse power. Now problems were *shared*.

Nobody at Ford understood that better than Mark Fields, who would take over as CEO when Mulally retired in 2014.

"I guess fortunately," Fields told me, "our business started deteriorating well before the financial crisis. It's kind of played out that we had the foresight to go out and get all the financing. But it was just timing. We went into the soup first. Although we never got to the point where we were biting our fingernails because we were worried we were going to run out of money or not be able to make the payroll that month. But it was definitely harrowing."

The One Ford plan was a deeply American thing for Mulally to implement. It required a sophisticated, quietly calculating hayseed to pull it off. At some fundamental level, Mulally understood this essential thing about himself: that his appearance was a useful ruse, providing cover for radical action if it was needed. And his actions were radical. From the beginning, he didn't think that it *could* all go away, at Ford and in the auto industry more broadly—he knew he had landed in the middle of its *actually going away*.

Mulally pushed hard, but it was a cheerful push. In his entire tenure at Ford, he would never once be seen in a suit. At one point, according to Bryce Hoffman's 2013 account of Ford's revival, *American Icon: Alan Mulally and the Fight to Save Ford Motor Company*, Mulally's eventual heir, Mark Fields, was so sure that he was out of a job that he simply gave in to Mulally's mandate for radical managerial transparency and became the first car guy at Ford to label a vehicle troubled.

Fields—who with his Way Forward plan had begun to lay groundwork to streamline Ford's operations, such as by closing plants—tells a slightly different story. He was running Ford's U.S. operations at the time, and he wasn't sure he was screwed, even though he hadn't been elevated to the CEO's office.

"I wasn't pissed off," Fields said. "I had just gotten the job running the Americas. That was a big job, and we had a lot of things to do. We had to fix the business." But he decided to put aside a career of maneuvering through Ford's executive offices to do things Mulally's way.

"We were a culture where in any given meeting, we would focus on the ten things that were going wrong and maybe the one thing that was going right."

That was the old Ford, where managers focused on tearing each other down rather than figuring out how to maximize strengths. The law of the jungle ruled the company: kill or be killed. It didn't matter if you were picking up market share in Europe or expanding a foothold in China, because it was so much more advantageous to slaughter the guy whose new SUV was running behind in the United States. To make matters worse, the guy whose SUV was running behind would never admit that he had a problem; he would consider asking for help to be career suicide.

In Hoffman's book, Fields is depicted repeatedly as a swaggering New Jersey street fighter, who saw his destiny at Ford as a steady march of confrontation. It was the classic path to the top for an American male who wanted to make it big in the bare-knuckle business world of Detroit, where the expensive suits distracted the uninitiated from the boardroom blood sport.

Fields had lost his private-jet privileges when the cost of a weekend commute to Florida caught the attention of the media, but he was already getting accustomed to Mulally's quite different approach to doing things.

More important, Fields's resigned bravado endeared him to Mulally, who was new on the job when Fields flagged a car, the Ford Edge crossover, as "red"—very troubled. (Green and yellow were the other colors in Mulally's chromatic matrix of progress reports, updated weekly at the CEO's main Ford management meeting.)

Contrary to some accounts, Fields wasn't on the verge of packing it in at that point. He didn't see his problem car, which had an issue with its lift gate, the vehicle's rear hatch, as a perfect opportunity to go out in a blaze of glory.

"I was never ready to check out on the company," he told me. "I love the company. But I'm the kind of person who has the inability to accept defeat, and that's why I've gone for the messy assignments. So when Alan came in and we started the [regular business plan review, or BPR], we were coming from being a company where if you showed any weakness, you must not be very competent, and we can get somebody else."

And that led to a classic problem of corporate America, according to Fields: "Things were suppressed." So Fields decided to do something about that.

There was the Edge problem, which Fields's launch team had alerted him to. Then the prep team for the BPR came in, and when they showed him his presentation materials, Edge was marked green. "It was about a month after Alan came in, December, and we wanted to ship the vehicles, because we realize the revenue when the vehicle leaves the plant."

Fields tells the tale as if it happened yesterday, perhaps internally amused that the chutzpah that had gotten him to the top at Ford, and that some thought might be his undoing, actually kicked in at exactly the right time.

"I said, 'Guys, it's *not* green. We're holding the vehicles at the plant.'" But there was a plan, his team said. Fields didn't need to go into the BPR with a red on his charts.

"Is it a defined plan?" Fields asked. He wanted to understand the specific steps, so that if Mulally asked for details, he could lay them out. The answer was no.

"Then we've got to call it red."

Fields grinned when he got to the next part. "There was dead silence. They all wanted to make the boss look good. They wanted to know I really wanted to do this."

Fields patiently explained that Ford had a new leader and what he wanted above all was transparency. "We can't hide a secret," Fields said. "Code it red."

There were about twenty people assembled around the conference room table for the BPR, and other executives were videoconferencing in from around the world, from Shanghai, Rome, South America. Fields, because of his position and responsibility for North America, went first. After a few minutes, he got to his launch chart.

"It showed bright red for Edge." While he was recounting this story, I could tell that he had learned to appreciate the value of a critical moment for Ford as the financial crisis was unfolding. He could have said simply "red," but he said "bright red."

It was that kind of red. On few occasions has the management culture of a 100-year-old company been transformed by one man's embrace of a primary color.

"You could hear a pin drop," he said. "I could actually feel some of the chairs around me start to move away, because two guys in black trench coats are going to come in and haul me out."

But they didn't haul him out. Instead, Mulally said, "Mark, thanks for your transparency."

"And the following week," Fields recollected, "all the charts showed up like rainbows."

Fields's own transformation continued, and much of it could be chalked up to his own appetite to learn from the genial former Boeing exec, who greeted everyone with a smile but still calculated the odds in the back of his mind.

"What I learned from Alan is the power of positive leadership," Fields told me. "How do you get the best out of people in really dire situations? He has that skill that politicians have, to make you feel good about a good situation, or a crappy situation, or anything in between."

The Mark Fields of 2016, the Ford CEO presiding over record sales quarters for the carmaker and steering the company back to Le Mans, had become a suave operator, a smooth study in *usually* saying the right thing, refusing to withhold truly bad news, and deploying wit instead of a belligerent attitude. When I told him I had moved to New Jersey, he immediately asked, "What exit?" referring to the Garden State Parkway, a tollway that runs diagonally through the state, forming a socioeconomic spine. It's the classic inside joke for Jersey natives, (Fields grew up in Paramus).

Like Mulally, Fields engages warmly with journalists, whereas a decade earlier he might have seen them as foes. When I chatted with him at the offices of *Business Insider* in New York in 2016, around the time of the New York International Auto Show and the U.S. auto industry's victory lap after the epic sales of 2015, Fields was more than happy to engage in some ribbing banter about Lincoln head Kumar Galhotra and the transformation of the executive from stern-faced engineer to a smiling, mellow, stylish diplomat. Fields had been an executive who thought about himself first, but Mulally taught him to think about the Ford family—from the factory floor to the heirs to the original Ford fortune. Groomed in a firestorm during the financial crisis, Fields had studied under the best. Mulally's work at Ford is now widely regarded as one of the most impressive rescue missions in the history of American business. It did all nearly go away. A guy from Kansas prevented Armageddon in Motown. And Fields was clear that just because the industry had recovered was no justification for easing back on the throttle.

"My grandmother went through the Great Depression. And we went through our own Great Recession and our own cathartic restructuring of the business. That isn't lost on us. There's no time to sit back and say, 'Hey, let's go have a beer and slack off for a month.'"

Fields called it staying "riveted" on the business. Mulally's ongoing legacy has inspired this philosophy, this kind of focus, and this kind of shared responsibility at Ford.

"We're proud that we didn't take the bailout money," Fields said. "We're proud we did this on our own."

Without Mulally, there would have been no Ford, or at least no Ford as America had grown to know it.

All this management theory put into practice needed to be more than just a big thought experiment. It needed to work at the level of transforming Ford's corporate culture. The carmaker's portfolio of cars and trucks also had to be improved. Coming out of the financial crisis, Ford unquestionably had the best lineup of vehicles in the industry, among mass-market automakers, gathered under a single brand. GM would also come out of bankruptcy selling an excellent range of vehicles—the revival of Buick was particularly impressive—but GM was still a company of several brands, not a single brand. (Ford also had Lincoln and Mercury, but those nameplates weren't Mulally's priority, in the beginning, and left to his own devices, he probably would have ditched them.)

I went to Ford's West Coast design center in Irvine, California, several times right after the carnage from the financial crisis had begun to abate and saw One Ford in the flesh. I also saw the consequences of the crisis: Ford had occupied the entire building, just off the freeway, when it had owned Jaguar, Land Rover, Volvo, and Aston Martin. But by the time I dropped in, those premium brands had been sold off, and half the building was leased to Taco Bell. The luxury brands were leftovers from the Nasser years, and Ford had sold them, one by one or in pairs (as with Jaguar and Land Rover), to clarify its portfolio and quit wasting money developing and supporting those snazzy nameplates.

One event in Irvine centered on the Fiesta, an inexpensive small car; Ford had enjoyed success with the Fiesta in Europe and had decided to make a bigger push for it in the United States, where gas prices were high and incomes had been reduced if not destroyed. Another event centered on the new Ford Taurus, a nameplate Mulally himself had asked to have brought back. This was a full-size four-door that was aimed squarely at families.

By 2010, Ford was in a solid position with the core products. That year a hybrid version of the Fusion sedan would win the prestigious North American Car of the Year award at the Detroit auto show. Later that year I would get a good look at One Ford in action, when I made my annual visit to the Los Angeles auto show in November. Displaying a range from small cars to big trucks, and with plenty of Mustangs on the floor as a reminder that Ford hadn't abandoned its high-performance efforts, the car-maker proved it could build just about anything a customer might want. If you needed a car or a truck or a big truck or a hybrid, Ford had you covered.

This sort of product perfection is rare in the auto industry. (Volkswagen, for one, had for years been trying to stage a come-back in the U.S. market and kept getting its mix of cars and SUVs wrong.) And it never lasts, as models come to the middle of their market cycles and often have to wait for full-on redesigns, sub-sisting instead on what carmakers call "refreshes." But at Ford, the stars aligned as the U.S. market began its slow recovery from a cratered annual sales number of 10 million after the financial crisis. And even as the market improved and gas prices dropped, and as customers were less interested in Fiestas and Fusions, shift-ing back to Explorer SUVs and F-150 pickups, Ford was prepared to take ongoing risks.

A big one was the risky redesign of the F-150, Ford's undisputed cash cow, in 2015. The F-150—sometimes called the "F-Series," an evocation of its existence in the U.S. market for four decades encompassing changes in the numbers associated with its name and the addition of larger pickups—accounted for nearly 800,000 vehicle sales in 2015. Even in years when the market isn't epically strong, the F-150 wins the sales crown. It has been America's top seller for thirty-four years in a row, through multiple recessions and downturns and even one near-depression. It's almost always the best-selling vehicle every month, although it was briefly dethroned in May 2008, when the Toyota Camry and Corolla and the Honda Civic captured more buyers. No one was surprised by this, given the economic conditions at the time, but the vulnerability of Ford's most important vehicle would spur a major change in how it was put together.

The federal government also played a role, by requiring that automakers raise their CAFE standards starting in 2017 and stretching into 2021. The National Highway Traffic Safety Administration, in cooperation with the Environmental Protection Agency, established that the new standard across an automaker's fleet would have to rise to forty-one miles per gallon.

Full-size pickups don't get anywhere near forty-one miles per gallon. The F-150, in its popular eight-cylinder-engine versions, doesn't even get twenty. The automakers have some options here. One is to build more of what they often derisively refer to as "compliance" vehicles—fuel-sipping small cars, hybrids, and electric cars—which collectively raise their CAFE numbers but unfortunately don't sell very well and can cost more to build than they bring in when they do sell.

The argument in the industry is that the government is forcing it to build higher-MPG, lower-emissions vehicles to satisfy a mandated number, but that customers don't want and won't buy those vehicles, defeating the purpose of raising the CAFE standards in the first place. Smaller engines in larger vehicles, an obvious work-around, aren't an option, because the buyers of big trucks and SUVs want power—and not just to accelerate on freeways but so that they can use their vehicles to tow trailers and boats.

The best solution, apart from petitioning the government to extend the CAFE deadlines (something the automakers did actively in 2015 and 2016), is to develop new engines that achieve higher MPG ratings without sacrificing power, and reducing the weight of vehicles, taking advantage of a basic rule of physics that says an engine will consume less gas if it has to move less weight around.

Ford tackled the problem using both of those tactics. Interestingly, the payoff would help lead to the new GT that was revealed at the 2015 Detroit auto show—a car that was about as far from being a "compliance" effort as any ever produced.

The huge bet that One Ford enabled was the redesign of the F-150 to include more lightweight aluminum than the heavier steel used previously. The huge risk was that F-150 buyers wouldn't accept that a truck made of lighter material would be able to stand up to the punishment that F-150s routinely absorb. Owners want to be able, without worry, to throw *anything* into the bed of their Ford trucks. And anything could mean, say, an antique sideboard, bales of hay, the rusted cast-iron engine of an old Ford truck, a few hundred pounds of dirt, a harvest of tomatoes, eight bags of soccer balls, three dogs, a chopped-down and sectioned oak tree, six Marshall 100-watt amps, or twenty-five cinder blocks. Would the new aluminum-bodied truck be able to take it?

The lighter material was a risk-abatement strategy: Ford needed to be able to continue to sell its very profitable F-150 in massive numbers and to avoid offsetting its lower fuel economy by adding a bunch of Fiestas to the fleet. Some owners might doubt the plan, but Ford had to power through their reservations and convince them that the new F-150 could get the job—*any job*—done. One clever way the company addressed this anxiety was by calling the new aluminum alloy used for the pickup "military grade." The appellation was accurate, given that the chosen aluminum alloy had been defined as military grade for years. Any skeptic might have asked whether "military grade" meant "war-zone grade," and Ford would have answered no, but the notion that the mighty F-150 would be made of the same flimsy, crushable stuff as a Bud Light can was dispelled.

The launch of the new truck wasn't without problems. The assembly lines had to be revamped to bolt the new aluminum components together, whereas with the old truck welding was used. There weren't enough F-150s, with enough of the extras that truck buyers require, to satisfy demand, so Ford had to play catch-up. But by spring of 2016 the risk had paid off, as F-150 sales continued to make their historic contribution to Ford's bottom line—and perhaps more important, customers had few complaints about the new truck.

Prior to rolling out the aluminum F-150, Ford developed a new engine technology, also intended to make the new CAFE standards easier to meet. Turbocharging had been popular in the U.S. market in the 1980s, but it was mainly provided by European automakers. Turbos were synonymous with Saab and Volvo, and Porsche had convinced enthusiasts that turbos were the way to go to extract more power from smaller engines (a good thing, as a smaller engine improves handling and speed). But American automakers shied away from the technology, preferring to put big V-8s in their trucks and SUVs, while dropping smaller V-6 engines into the midsize cars and four-cylinder motors into the compacts. These engines were simpler to build without the addition of the turbocharger, which uses exhaust gas to spin a turbine that compresses intake air before feeding it to the combustion chambers, thereby enriching the fuel-air mixture and yielding more power per cylinder. Presto! A smaller displacement V-6 can thereby match a V-8.

The new CAFE standards meant V-8s couldn't make up as large a portion of the automakers' fleets as they did previously, so Ford needed to engineer a way to achieve better fuel efficiency without compromising power.

The solution was a new generation of turbocharged V-6 motors that Ford dubbed EcoBoost ("boost" is the technical term for how much extra power the turbocharger is adding to the engine's output, and some cars actually include a gauge so that drivers can monitor it). Turbos have two drawbacks. One is that the additional power they deliver can take a few seconds to develop before it becomes available to the drive wheels as rotational energy, called "torque." This is the dreaded "turbo lag." The second is that turbos create heat, which is the enemy of engines: old turbos had a tendency to get so hot that they baked lubricants into their compressor blades and burned out seals: after a while, they leaked and needed to be overhauled.

EcoBoost promised to turn all the old turbo anxieties into fading memories—and in execution, the new engines lived up to their ambitions. They were twin-scroll turbochargers, more complicated than the older types of turbos but capable of applying the principles of turbo compression more efficiently, which when combined with direct-fuel injection made for better MPG ratings and far less turbo lag.

The motors were put into F-150s and won over customers who formerly would have bought only pickups with a V-8. The EcoBoost technology also showed up in smaller cars with four-cylinder engines, providing snappy acceleration along the lines of that found in sports cars. But it was on the track that the EcoBoost technology truly made its mark.

It was an immediate success. In January 2015, Chip Ganassi Racing—a frequent partner with Ford—won the Rolex 24 at Daytona, the American race that most closely resembles Le Mans, with a prototype car using a 3.5-liter EcoBoost V-6 built by Roush Yates Racing Engines. That engine normally cranks out 365 horsepower, but Roush Yates was able to jack it up to 600.

At the time, it might have seemed to racing fans that Ford was just experimenting with a new engine. Automakers do it all the time. But the company had something much bigger in mind.

Chapter 3

Behold the New GT

Like many impressive creations, the new GT wasn't exactly born—it was coaxed to life, slowly and haltingly at first, and then with the accelerator pedal jammed to the floor.

Mark Fields had always wanted to build a true successor to the GT40, a completely new car, not an homage like the GTs of 2004 to 2006. As much as the fiftieth anniversary of the Le Mans win presented the perfect opportunity, Ford's recovery from the financial crisis made the timing difficult.

For Ford, going back to Le Mans with a Mustang would have been a lot easier. Scott Atherton, the president of the International Motor Sports Association (IMSA)—sports-car racing's governing body in North America—told me the Le Mans comeback was originally supposed to be Mustang-based. Raj Nair, Ford's chief technical officer and the final decision-maker for the GT racing and road-car program, said the same thing. That would have made sense. There are Mustangs that can be upgraded to endurance-race worthiness, with a setup similar to what Corvette Racing had run in the IMSA series and had used to win Le Mans: a big V-8 up front, rear-wheel drive out back, and a downforce wing rising from the trunk lid.

There also wouldn't have been issues with satisfying the re-quirements of both IMSA and the Fédération Internationale de l'Automobile (or FIA, the overseer of European motorsports), which stipulate that cars in the GT racing classes have road-going counterparts. (The reason for this is that endurance race cars are supposed to be test beds for technologies that ordinary consum-ers will someday experience.) Ford had been building Mustangs since 1965. The car was already an established racing platform, although Ford didn't have a racing team that enjoyed the full sup-port, funding, and sponsorship of the entire Ford Performance organization—what's known in racing as a factory team. That could have been corrected easily; there was no shortage of avail-able high-performance Mustang packages. Raj Nair told me much later that there had indeed been discussion about returning to Le Mans in 2015 with a Mustang to celebrate the fiftieth anniversary of the iconic "pony car." But for Ford, a Le Mans Mustang would have been a huge missed chance.

At the highest executive level, Ford decided in late 2014 to scrap the Mustang idea and take the plunge with a brand-new supercar. It would be the centerpiece of an entire division of the automaker, showcasing the fastest, the most exciting, and the most exotic: Ford Performance.

And yet it made sense to worry about the GT's Le Mans chances just a bit, given that the Ferrari 488, with 606 horsepower, had an extra dollop of grunt. Its predecessor, the 458, was also one of the premier sports cars on earth—and a familiar racing weapon, running in both IMSA and FIA World Endurance Champion-ship events for years. It was a reminder that although Ford had NASCAR and was no stranger to racing, Ferrari had already staked out territory that the new GT would be attempting to storm.

I had driven the road version of the 488, and also several versions of the Chevrolet Corvette, including the pride of the Bowling

Green, Kentucky, factory, the Z06—Chevy's own front-engine supercar—and the C7 Stingray, the seventh generation of the iconic Vette. The Z06 has a 650-horsepower motor and is one of the most mentally demanding cars I've ever driven. It has so much power, available anytime you want it, that it's hard to take it easy, even when you're just cruising around. The Stingray, on the other hand, was simply magnificent, with a 455-horsepower V-8 that sounds like eight angry angels with a jones for speed.

The C7.R sat in between and was given the bespoke race-car treatment by Pratt & Miller, a Michigan-based shop that has been hooked up with Chevy for almost a decade. Pratt & Miller had constructed a 491-horsepower machine that had been getting it done on the track since 2013. The C7.R was also the defending Le Mans champ from 2015. Together, Pratt & Miller and Chevy had won Le Mans eight times.

It's fair to say that because of its record, General Motors saw Ford as something of an arriviste in its return to Le Mans. But as good as the Vettes had been, it was also clear that in 2016, a change was afoot in sports-car racing, shifting the balance of power back toward mid-engine cars in the old GT40 legacy and away from front-engine and rear-engine designs. In fact, it was strongly rumored that Chevy was going to create a mid-engine Corvette, and I have to believe that the project was driven in part by what Ford had done with the GT.

In Dearborn, the GT started in a basement, with a mysterious sign, a key, and a team of designers who, once the cover had been pulled off their baby, were shocked that they'd been able to keep it secret, right up until the car was revealed in Detroit.

"For once, it's true," Moray Callum told me, with a guffaw, when I talked to him in early 2016, right after the new GT's racing debut at the Rolex 24 at Daytona, a few months before the road car would be available for preorders.

Callum, who is Scottish, heads up Ford design. He's from a car-design family. His older brother, Ian, dictates the look of Jaguars and staged his own triumph in late 2015, with the debut of Jag's first-ever SUV, the gorgeous F-PACE.

Moray Callum doesn't exactly look or act the part of a car designer. His nature is cheerful, not intense or austere. He dresses unpretentiously, forgoing the sleek black suits, gigantic and costly wristwatches, and severe eyeglasses that most auto-industry observers associate with the more artsy employees of the business. He originally wanted to be a veterinarian, before a season working on a farm convinced him to pursue another calling. First he tried architecture and then he found car design.

Callum landed at Ford in 1995, after stints with Chrysler and the French automaker Peugeot. He worked for J Mays, a car designer's car designer. Mays had crafted the revived Beetle for Volkswagen, oversaw the rehabilitation of Audi, and conceived a retro-modern Thunderbird for Ford. In 2001 Callum took over design for Mazda (Ford and Mazda had a partnership from 1979 until the financial crisis forced a split in 2010), where one of his first responsibilities was a revamp of the beloved MX-5 Miata roadster. He has, to say the least, been around the design block a few times, and for a kid who initially wanted to heal animals and then create buildings, it's been a tremendous ride. Talking to him, you can tell he's relished every minute of the job. Nearly sixty by the time the Le Mans fiftieth anniversary rolled around, he would get to see a design he dreamed up make a run for renewed glory on a course that has mythical meaning for the Ford Motor Company.

That he was chuckling about how the GT was created, rather than shedding tears, was a testament to his own lineage.

"The Scottish are a nation of engineers," Ian Callum told the *New York Times* in 2006. "But they are very creative engineers. They seem dour, but underneath they are quite romantic."

Romance is all well and good, but secrecy was of the essence for the GT. It was, however, an offbeat sort of secrecy, more garage band than arena rock, more skunkworks than high-profile industrial undertaking. If the massive River Rouge plant signified Henry Ford's ambition and defined Ford during the automaker's mid-century heyday—then the mysterious, low-key GT studio defined how Ford wanted to develop this most exciting of post-financial-crisis cars.

"We kept it quiet, for obvious reasons," Callum told me. "Very few people knew what was going on, and a lot of executives didn't see the car until the day of the Detroit show."

For all practical purposes, Ford designed one of its most striking, exotic, historic, and widely anticipated (not to mention rapturously received) cars in the automotive equivalent of a broom closet.

"We formed a very small team, and we literally put them in the basement of our Product Development Center, all the way in the back, where nobody ever goes," Callum said.

"It had been used for milling and storage," he said, before confessing that he and his small team of designers had engaged in a "little bit of subterfuge" to keep the GT under wraps and away from prying eyes as it was perfected.

The ruse went all the way to top, where Mark Fields himself enjoyed all the spy-movie secrecy.

Then there was the sign.

"We put a printed sign on a piece of eight-and-a-half-by-eleven paper, and it said something mundane like 'Past Model Parts Depot,'" Fields said. "And then we challenged the team to come up with a successor."

Beyond the sign and the need-to-know-basis security, the design process also included waiting until Sundays to wheel the car out from the basement so it could be studied under natural light.

According to Christopher Svensson, Ford's design director for the Americas, design reviews were started at seven o'clock in the evening and went on until eleven.

And then there was the key.

Callum seemed to think this small detail was the most hilarious aspect of the entire double top-secret design process for the GT.

"It was *physically* a metal key," he said, chuckling, clearly amused that a vehicle as high-tech as the GT—it's made almost entirely of carbon fiber, and the fabrication techniques that went into building it allowed for some fairly outlandish curves and shapes—would be guarded by what was the state of the art for security in 1930.

The key was later replaced by security cards, but the birthplace of the GT wasn't similarly upgraded.

Ford released a video of the studio in 2015. Anyone expecting a tour of a state-of-the-art facility, full of chic people sipping lattes and muttering about aesthetics while debating curves and scoops, would have been greatly disappointed. The top-secret GT studio was, for one thing, crowded. There wasn't much room for the camera to navigate the gloomy, grungy space, and Callum and his design team were packed in with foam mock-ups, clay models, rolling bulletin boards covered with conceptual renderings and engineering studies, various bits and pieces that would go into the finished car, and the obligatory computer equipment to envision and execute the GT.

It looked far more like a garage set up for hot-rodding on a semi-pro scale than a state-of-the art design mecca, a Motown equivalent of Ford's lovely and well-equipped facility in southern California.

In Dearborn, there was a buzzing sense that Callum and his guys were up to something. And the team stoked the impression that it had something under wraps—quite literally. Callum recounted a holiday party at which various Ford designers created snowmen to show off their design chops.

"Ours was in the corner," he recalled. "It was covered by a sheet, and it had a padlock on it."

That was a clear signal that Callum's team probably wasn't creating a new Explorer. There was a fresh and exciting car on the horizon, and figuring out what it would be was left to the deductive faculties of Ford employees. A little math, of course, and an ear to the grapevine, a finger on the thrum of the rumor mill, would have led to reasonable guesses about a Le Mans car. What savvy scrutinizers of Callum's secret design workshop couldn't know was that the GT was being developed simultaneously as a road car and a race car. (In an interesting modern-day twist, among the few people in the know was a small group of Microsoft Xbox video-game designers, who were working to include the GT in the *Forza Motorsport 6* update, which came out in 2016.)

Multimatic Motorsports, Ford Performance's race-car builder, would bolt together two machines north of the U.S.–Canadian border, near Toronto, a few hours from Detroit by car, and two others in England, for the European side of the Le Mans campaign. The demands of constructing a race car are significantly different from those of creating a road car. For example, a race car needs to be easy to take apart, so that it can be repaired as quickly as possible, and in some cases race cars have less-sophisticated components than their road-car counterparts, depending on the regulations of the governing body of the series they compete in.

Multimatic had expertise with carbon-fiber fabrication, a vital aspect of modern race-car and supercar production. Light but strong, carbon fiber is an ideal material to use for constructing racing vehicles. It's essentially threads of carbon glued together in tidy fashion with a polymer, then treated to create a reinforced plastic material that can be shaped into just about anything, from a smartphone case to a supercar body panel. Multimatic had gotten skilled at carbon-fiber fabrication from building high-performance race cars, most of which are now made of the stuff. The advantages of carbon fiber are numerous: it's ten times stronger than aluminum and eight times stronger than steel, can be sculpted into a variety of shapes, resists heat and corrosion very effectively, and doesn't fatigue as easily as other materials, thanks to its flexibility. For years, automakers have tried to figure out how to use it in more mainstream vehicles, but carbon fiber, at around twelve dollars a pound, is also extremely expensive; aluminum is only about two dollars per pound, and steel is less than a dollar. For that reason, high-end road cars often use aluminum, while mass-market vehicles are made with good old-fashioned steel.

Only 500 GTs for the road and four for the track would initially be built, with two racing in North America and two in Europe. The car would be exceptionally rare, and that low production number, along with the steep price tag, signaled that although Ford was creating the race cars and road cars at the same time, the GT was first and foremost a competitive machine, committed to race in both the United States and Europe until 2019. Every other vehicle that it would race against in 2016 would be built (in some cases had been built) in far greater numbers for the road and would not be so strictly limited in terms of total production.

Interestingly, although the new GT was created under these unusual conditions, it wasn't a tense or difficult process. Under the circumstances, this was remarkable.

"It was less of a challenge," Callum said, "than designing, say, the next-generation Fiesta"—that small Ford vehicle I had checked out in Irvine several years before. An inexpensive mass-market car like that has to be designed and built to a price point, engineered for the production of hundreds of thousands of units in many different countries. When designing such a vehicle, you're always deciding what not to do.

The GT was different. "We tried to stretch the limits as much as possible," Callum said.

He got the nod to design the supercar about eighteen months before its scheduled debut at the Detroit show in January 2015. "It was a great privilege," Callum said, but he quickly added that he didn't sweat the process of assembling the team, nor did he cherry-pick a band of specialists to gather a GT Special Forces unit. "We had people fresh out of design school, and we had people with a lot of experience. What we were seeking was some naïveté. And in the end it was the most collaborative project of my career."

Such a laid-back approach didn't diminish the daunting task ahead. "The original Le Mans–winning GT is one car that we look back on and say, 'We got everything right,'" he said.

Once design began in earnest, the requirement of making the 2016 deadline for Le Mans entry drove everything. Callum had just over a year to create something breathtaking. But the work went fast. The ideas were in place, the grand theories had been cultivated in advance, and so it all came down to execution. That was all it took to create a machine that would dazzle at an epic level.

Three months in, Callum and the GT team had solidified the basic design theme. The new GT had to be stunning, but it also had to evoke the GT40—without repeating the look of the mid-2000s GT—and it had to be an effective race car. "The racing rules helped us," he said. "What the racing guys wanted was what we wanted."

That included even the most exotic aspects of the GT: signature "flying buttress" wings that curved down from the rear roofline to the back wheels; Callum called these wings a "natural choice."

"It came in early," he recalled. So did the overall aerodynamic layout of the car.

Team member Garen Nicoghosian, who oversaw the exterior design of the car, essentially envisioned the GT as a combination of machine and sculpture, whose first job was to interact dynami-cally with the atmosphere. He described the body of the car to *Hot Rod Network* as a "collection of items that collect air, avoid air, or make better use of air." Even the doughnut-shaped taillights are designed to vent air as it rushes over, around, and through the GT.

The familiar concept of the sports car as work of art was, in this case, derived directly from history. Callum noted that the original GT40, although it has been characterized as more of a blunt, industrial instrument than the Ferrari it trounced in the 1960s, was sculptural.

The Le Mans–winning 1960s cars were a combination of smoothly crafted front ends and harshly rectangular rears, low and wide. Even today, they cut a striking image, one of brute power wrapped in a taut skin: the muscles are slablike, the sinews tight.

The GT40 of the 1960s was considered gorgeous by some but an American brute by others. Today, given its size and scale, it doesn't look especially crude. But whatever beauty it might have possessed in rough form in 1965 and '66 was far surpassed by the Italians and their aesthetic flair later in that decade and the one to follow. Ironically, even though Ford ended Ferrari's reign at Le Mans, it was Ford that retreated from the supercar era. There wouldn't be another GT until the early 2000s, and it was more rep-lica than aesthetic advance, although it did beat the performance of the GT40's titanic 7.0-liter V-8 engine with a more modern and compact 5.4-liter supercharged V-8. Otherwise, however, it lacked the old GT40's raw threat. The infamous British car journalist and erstwhile *Top Gear* host Jeremy Clarkson called it "civilized."

No one would have said that about the GT40. Chris Amon, the man who drove the winning 1966 Le Mans GT40 with Bruce McLaren, reminisced in 2016 about how the car nearly beat him to death. After a driving stint, he would immediately shed his sweat-soaked racing suit and have a shower.

The bottom line was that the GT40 was built to race, and to win Le Mans, and everything about it flowed from that purpose. Style and comfort were completely secondary. The follow-up GT was, in many respects, an homage to the original car, with modern creature comforts thrown in.

Callum called the new GT "a synergy of design theory and engineering," defusing one of the oldest disagreements in automotive history: that between designers coming up with outlandish creations and the guys who actually build the cars telling them that they need to dial it back.

Not much was dialed back on the GT. Even the engine was a no-compromise undertaking—although it isn't the screaming V-8 of a Ferrari 458, or the burbling, potent V-12 of a Lamborghini Aventador.

Instead, the new GT, stunning on the outside, is under the hood an advertisement for Ford's shift to turbocharged power plants. The beauty of a turbo engine, especially in a race car, is that it adds less weight overall than a supercharger, which requires the engine, rather than exhaust gases, to drive the increase in air pressure.

The drawback is heat: turbos get hot—extremely hot. So the air has to be cooled, as does the turbocharger itself. The trick with turbos on the racetrack is to make sure that they're durable enough to withstand, in the case of endurance racing, hours and hours of intense heat. In the GT, there are two turbochargers assisting the V-6 in cranking out 600 horsepower.

There are far more powerful supercars—they fall into an elevated class now referred to as "hypercar," or even "megacar," and can notch horsepower ratings of 1,000 and above—but the GT was designed, from the beginning, to race in the GT Le Mans class, not against those monster machines in the prototype class. In fact, of the cars in the GTE Pro class (GTLM in North America) for the 2016 season, only the Ferrari 488, itself featuring a turbocharged eight-cylinder mid-engine configuration, could be called a purpose-built race car, since all Ferraris have racing in their DNA. The rest of the field was made up of sports cars adapted for racing. That's not a knock on those designs—the Corvettes in the GTE Pro class performed fantastically well in sports-car racing against the Ferrari 488's predecessor, the 458. But like the GTs of the 1960s, the new cars were created with the track in mind. Not many people would get to keep one in the garage. By contrast, Ferrari sells some 7,000 cars a year (although most are not the mid-engine supercars).

When Ford first unveiled the GT in Detroit in January 2015, it didn't say anything about the cost or how many road cars it would be making. These details it revealed at the Chicago Auto Show in February: the new GT was going to cost in the mid-$400,000s, and Ford would be making 500 of them, 250 a year for two years. And the company would be scrupulous about who got to enjoy the unique pleasure of parting with all that money to buy one. In April 2016, Ford announced that it would be accepting applications for GT ownership over the following month, via a special website that featured a "configurator," which enabled prospective buyers to spec out their cars, choosing exterior colors, interior setups, wheels, and even the color of racing stripes.

It was a savvy idea. When the application period closed on May 12, Ford had received 6,506 fully completed applications to purchase the superhot supercar, and almost 200,000 people had used the configurator. (The car was so successful that Ford extended production for an additional two years, making the announcement in mid-August. Year three would address the waiting list from the initial application process, while year four would allow for reapplications. The entire process would also enable Ford to keep racing for three years after the debut.)

"We're excited by the amount of enthusiasm fans are showing for the new Ford GT," said Dave Pericak in a press release. And the fans were showing plenty of enthusiasm. Hundreds of potential buyers submitted videos with their applications, and many stressed their social-media reach in addition to showing how they'd use the car—whether to drive around town, like eGarage, whose video showed a GT being used to run errands with a baby in the passenger seat; take it on the track, like Brooks Weisblat, owner of DragTimes.com; or make it part of a large collection, like John Kiely and his father, Jack Kiely, who run a construction business in Long Branch, New Jersey.

It was generally assumed the fix was in for certain VIPs to jump to the head of the buying list. But Henry Ford III, the great-great-grandson of Henry Ford himself and the marketing director for Ford's Performance division, told me that the company was starting with as level a playing field as possible for future GT ownership. Prospective buyers had to fill out an extensive questionnaire as part of their application, answering questions about whether they were collectors, or owners of a current Ford GT or any Ford, whether they did business with the automaker or were involved in Ford-affiliated charities, and whether they considered themselves as "an influencer of public opinion." From the application, which inquired whether the prospective buyer held a motorsports sanctioning-body competition license, it seemed clear that Ford wanted people who didn't just drive the car but used all its abilities. Additionally, buyers had to agree not to sell their car for a quick profit.

Henry Ford III is the embodiment of trustworthiness. He has a bright, uncomplicated, Midwestern look—before he joined the family business, he spent some time as a teacher, and you can tell he was probably well liked by his students. His blond hair isn't worn in a fancy cut, and I've never seen him wearing anything more fashionable than a polo shirt and a pair of slacks. He's tall, but he doesn't lord it over anybody, and when he talks, you can tell he's smart—and also sharp enough to use straightforward English, never veering into business-speak.

But Henry III, like all Fords, does possess some formidable diplomatic skills. He stressed that initial consideration for sales would be given to existing Ford GT owners (about 10,000 cars of the previous version had been produced), as well as well-known owners of Ford's other high-performance cars. None of this was unreasonable. It's standard procedure among the world's supercar manufacturers. Most of the people offered the opportunity to buy Ferrari supercars are existing Ferrari owners—and this is likewise the case for the more exotic versions of Porsches and Lamborghinis. There are exceptions: The Audi R8 is produced in decent enough numbers that just about anyone can buy into being Tony Stark, the billionaire playboy superhero played by Robert Downey Jr. in the Iron Man franchise. And certain bargain supercars, like the Corvette Z06 and the Nissan GT-R (affectionately labeled "Godzilla" by enthusiasts), turn heads owing to their reputations and looks, not because spotting one on the freeway is a rare event.

Henry III was certainly proud of the new GT. "It sends a chill up my spine," he said, when I asked him about going back to Le Mans. But he also expressed awe at what Callum and his team, as well as the Ford Performance engineering group, had pulled off with the GT.

"It really has been the highlight of my career to work side by side with the designers and engineers," he said. "They created a masterpiece. Every time I see the car, I take a step back."

Effectively, however, not one but *two* masterpieces were created at the same time. And they were not tortured productions. There were no glitches or setbacks for Callum and his design team, although, because the new GT would be both a race car and road car, some compromises would be required, mainly for the road-going GT. (The racer would be stripped down and highly customized, with few creature comforts.) The up-swinging scissor doors required that the air-conditioning and heating vents be positioned in an unusual way, but as Amko Leenarts, Ford's Netherlands-born interior design director, explained to me, it wasn't especially difficult to develop the cockpit for the two-seater. He echoed Callum's comment that with something as focused as a supercar, much of the design takes care of itself, owing to the obvious spatial constraints that the designers are presented with. Additionally, there's an assumption that a $400,000-plus car will contain lots of premium materials, but no potential customer expects a Rolls-Royce when he or she slips inside.

One of the few surprises in store for eventual GT owners was what Multimatic vice president Larry Holt—an elusive man with a wild mane of curly gray hair, who was handling the simultaneous engineering of the GT road and race cars—called its "cozy" driver and passenger compartment, in a January 2016 interview with *Car* magazine. Anyone who has ever been in a Corvette Stingray, a Lamborghini Huracán, a Ferrari supercar, or even a Mazda Miata will tell you that a two-seater isn't about creature comforts. But with the Ford GT, there was an additional wrinkle: although Callum and his designers had been able to go for the dramatic with the exterior, the interior's scale would have to be more purposeful. The ultimate mission of the car, in the end, was to accommodate *one* driver and to go fast. So Multimatic and Ford Performance used what Holt told *Car* was the smallest interior on the market in 2014, in the United States or Europe, as their benchmark: the ultra-snug Lotus Elise, a roadster that's twelve and a half feet long and weighs less than 2,000 pounds.

A Le Mans car has to be designed in a way that makes it easy to take apart and easy to put back together. All the aerodynamic elements need to be swappable, as does the gearbox. Brakes must be able to be changed in a matter of minutes (typically, the pads— the parts that fit inside calipers to squeeze down on alloy disks to slow the car from 200-plus miles per hour to 50—might be changed once or twice over twenty-four hours). Engine failure is much harder to manage—it can be done, although it's generally fatal for winning. A blown engine usually means retiring the car.

A supercar for normal public motorways and freeways isn't executed in the same way. As Raj Nair noted in a Ford video during the Le Mans lead-up, you built a race car from the tires up, starting with the point in contact with the track surface. "What do the tires want?" Nair asked.

A consumer supercar, Nair said, is designed around what the owners expect, and even though supercars used to be uncomfortable, those days are long gone. I've driven numerous supercars, and all the modern ones have modes that enable you to drive your Audi R8 or McLaren 675LT as if it were a Honda Accord. You can flip a switch and unleash the beast, but anyone who drops between $200,000 and upwards of a million and change on a supercar doesn't want to be squashed into a stiff racing seat, thinly upholstered with fine leather but entirely lacking in padding. He or she also doesn't want to be made to scrimp on infotainment. There should be more than two speakers and an AM/FM radio—much, much more. GPS navigation is a given. That supercars are sometimes called "GTs" is a bit of a misnomer, because a proper GT—a *gran turismo* or "grand touring" car—has a backseat and the engine in the front. The buyers of mid-engine supercars used to be OK with tremendous discomfort. Now they want nothing more extreme on the inside than what they're used to in a daily driven BMW or Acura sports sedan.

Ford was lucky that the GT ended up being an unexpected breeze to design, engineer, and build, because the timetable, if the race car was going to be ready for a January debut in the United States, at the Rolex 24 at Daytona, was brutal. It would be OK if the supercar lagged the race car by a few months, as long as Ford could start auditioning buyers during the year. Multimatic could create some of the 250 model-year 2017 production vehicles that sold in 2016, rolling out into the light of day an actual operational, roadworthy GT, fully tested for safety and blessed by the governments of the United States and Europe.

But the race cars had to be ready for their first track tests in Canada by late spring 2015 and then for testing by late summer in the United States. Multimatic and Ford Performance nailed those milestones, which culminated in a full-day visit to Road Atlanta in Georgia on August 4. The GT was impressive.

"The first time we ran it was last spring," Multimatic test driver Scott Maxwell told auto journalist Gordon Kirby. "I've tested a lot of out-of-the-box cars and I was the first guy to drive the car. You always know pretty quickly, just through experience, whether it's going to be a dog or not. We weren't near the limit. We were just shaking it down but my gut told me that this was going to be a good car. It just felt right."

September would see the GTs flown to France, where FIA would check them out and determine whether any performance adjustments would be required to bring the cars in line with the other competitors in the GTE Pro class for the World Endurance Championship, of which Le Mans is the most prominent part. But it wouldn't be the GTs' first visit to France; tire maker Michelin explored the machine in June in order to get started developing the rubber that would quite literally meet the road at legendary racing venues on two continents.

The September FIA tests in France were the first indication that the GT Multimatic had built was extremely fast. Too fast, as it turned out, to enter the GTE Pro class without some tweaks. The racing authorities had two main ways to dial back the velocity of the swift new Fords. The first was fairly blunt: add weight. The GTs would come back to Europe forty-four pounds heavier, with lead-bar ballast weights bolted to the car by Ford and Chip Ganassi Racing and positioned in a way that wouldn't damage the cars' handling by unequally distributing the extra heft. The second was more specific to the turbocharged EcoBoost engine. Ford and Multimatic were instructed to reduce the car's boost, making it less powerful than what had been specified for IMSA competition in North America. Boost is the amount of additional air pressure the turbochargers are creating, which translates into extra engine power. By dialing it up or down, engineers can make their race car go faster or slower, which enables them to meet the performance standards for their racing class.

The subtext in Europe for Ford and Multimatic, and eventually Ford Chip Ganassi Racing, was that, as Holt told *Car* magazine, FIA didn't want a brand-new entrant to come "out of the box too hard." As a racing pro with plenty of experience, he understood that if the GTs performed poorly in Europe when the WEC season started in April 2016, they could get back some boost, lose some weight, or enjoy a combination of both.

The GT program was hitting its benchmarks, but it wasn't business as usual at Multimatic. A small contingent of engineers embedded with Ford would grow to dozens, working around the world. That was an advantage: the time differences enabled Multimatic to operate on a twenty-four-hour schedule, passing off responsibilities as the sun moved around the globe and the calendar closed in on the beginning of the IMSA and WEC seasons and marched inexorably toward Le Mans in June.

"This is a technological statement, taking on the best tech in the world," Larry Holt said at the time, making Ford's and Multimatic's objectives clear. Raj Nair echoed Holt's determination, insisting that GT had to be good as soon as it hit the track for the first time, because if it wasn't, it would be hard to make it good, much less great.

The first GT race cars to break cover and run outside didn't yet have their snazzy red-white-and-blue racing livery; they were a gloomy matte gray, almost charcoal. But the innovative shape was undeniable. And the car *worked* right away. It worked so well, in fact, that both the Ford and the Multimatic teams got nervous. It shouldn't have been that easy.

Ford had pushed its luck and knew it, but there had been no major issues. The company hadn't really built a true supercar before, although it had come close in 1995, with the GT90 concept car, a futuristic successor to the GT40 that, for a brief period, stoked some hopes about a Le Mans return. It never entered production, however. And while the EcoBoost engine had been raced by Ganassi in prototype-class cars, it had never been tested in sports-car competition, where the cars are heavier and handle differently, moving better through corners than the blistering-fast prototypes. But Le Mans in 2016 exerted an inexorable pull—it was the Gallic gravity well of deep history for Ford, epic and poetic in equal parts—and shaped Ford's priorities. The schedule was merciless, the pressure extreme, the demands immense, the opportunity for disaster and disappointment ever present. The fate of the entire company wasn't riding on the car, as it might have been with the new F-150, but the GT was a symbol to end all symbols: of Ford's determination, of its legacy, and of its revival.

On the marketing side, Ford was committed to using the new GT as a showcase for the technologies that it has developed. For Fields, a marketing guy at heart, it was a can't-miss opportunity to sell EcoBoost not just as a good fuel-economy option but also as one of the best engines in the world. It could deliver good mileage in a pickup truck, it could pep up a small car—and it could win the most grueling race in the world.

"It was all about challenging traditions," Fields told me, when I spoke to him at Le Mans in June. "The traditional approach would have been to put a big-ass V-8 in there, or let's do another V-12 and stuff it in. But [the team] came back and said that they could use a 3.5-liter EcoBoost engine that produces over 600 horsepower. And what that did for Moray and the team was that it gave the designers huge degrees of freedom, because the engine is so compact."

So the deliberate engineering choices led to a gorgeous yet functional design that few found anything to complain about. The car looked fantastic from every angle, with a front end that alluded to the legacy of past GT cars without being in their thrall. The lines then swept back to a compressed rear end, but with the wheels pushed out, providing an opening for Callum and his team to use the flying buttress, effectively an integrated wing. For over fifty years, cars have been trying to look like planes. The GT genuinely appeared as if it might be able to take flight.

But the car was specifically designed to do the opposite. Both the race car and the road car would need to use inverted lift—downforce—provided by the aerodynamics to stay stuck to the road or to the racecourse.

In automotive parlance, this is known as being "planted." The impression that you get when driving a car like this, with these technologies included in the design and engineering, is that the machine is controllable enough to push to the edge of being uncontrollable. That line of demarcation is what separates a performance car from one that's meant mainly to cruise around normally. Even a spirited sports sedan, such as the BMW 5 Series, will start to lurch and yaw and slip if you lay it into a corner too hard. This is the car's way of telling you it's had too much, and you need to dial it back, for safety's sake.

The GT forestalls that reckoning until the last possible moment. You'll never feel as if a supercar wants to roll over—because it doesn't. The worst possible driving outcome is that the rear tires lose grip and the car slides, a phenomenon known as "oversteer"—and one that enthusiasts and professional drivers favor.

The driver can accommodate for oversteer by steering in the opposite direction and allowing the car to drift through a corner, ever so slightly. The goal isn't to raise a glorious plume of tire smoke and drive the car sideways, as Jeremy Clarkson and his mates used to do on the hit BBC show *Top Gear*; that would cause the car's speed to decline precipitously. Rather, the idea is to give the driver some play, so that the car can handle more fluidly, thanks to the combination of tire oversteer and driver counter-steering to compensate for it. The car feels alive. Many pro drivers prefer this to the jarring lack of movement they can experience in all-wheel-drive race cars that don't approach unstable dynamics unless they're driven on unpaved surfaces, as in off-road rally races.

If a driver gets the counter-steering technique wrong, the masses of horsepower being channeled to the wheels from the engine will cause the car to over-rotate and spin. But the GT's mid-engine design helps to mitigate that possibility by placing the center of gravity at the center of the car, rather than parked out over the front wheels, as in a Corvette, or over the rear wheels, as in a Porsche 911. All other things being equal, a powerful mid-engine race car with rear-wheel-drive and a responsive transmission will outdrive everything else on a track.

That doesn't mean it will win every race, especially an endurance race. But it will handle better and as a result be faster—thanks to the driver's ability to tackle corners more aggressively—than competing layouts. It's a difficult balance that the racing team is trying to strike. Endurance races can be won by objectively slower cars that simply don't break down. But durable cars can also be blown off the track. The ideal Le Mans racer is tough enough and fast enough—but those "enoughs" are moving goalposts. You don't want to show up on race day with the toughest slow car, or the fastest unreliable one. In the 1960s, Ford struck this balance perfectly.

The new GT was a vast technological improvement over the GT40s of the 1960s and a leap beyond the GTs of the mid-2000s, which although capable of racing wouldn't have been competitive in the 2016 field at Le Mans, owing to their inability to generate adequate downforce. Obviously, there was no fooling around with turbochargers and six-cylinder engines fifty years ago. The GT40 was, by the standard set by the current GT Le Mans class of cars, utterly, completely, and defiantly old school. The mid-engine layout was the same, but the engine was a 486-horsepower, naturally aspirated V-8 with now-antiquated carburetors (Weber four-barrels, the state of the art for carburetors when Lyndon Johnson was in the White House). The top speed was stunning, nearly 200 miles per hour, but the zero-to-sixty time was only so-so by comparison with modern supercars: just over five seconds. In the 1960s, of course, that kind of acceleration would have drivers thinking about underwear changes, but in 2016, the new GT was punching it out in 3.3 seconds. The GT40's V-8 had to keep only 2,700 pounds moving at a bludgeoning pace once the car got going. The driver managed all that grunt with a four-speed transmission: he was squashed in low, between a pair of fuel tanks that held in excess of forty gallons of gas in total, and he surveyed a minimalist, industrial dashboard with analog gauges and switches to control the GT40's basic functions. The car was wide and low and fantastically uncomfortable—and only forty inches high, hence the "40" after the GT designation. A fire extinguisher rode shotgun. There was no domesticated, road-going version of this rude beast. What you saw was what you got. If you wanted to take it for a weekend spin in the country, you took out what had been raced on the track.

The driving was treacherous. Modern supercars and race cars have computers at their disposal to take the coarse edge off high-performance. The GT40 had nothing of the sort. There was no sophisticated modern brake technology, no traction control to sense when the rear wheels were being forced out by the power surging from that V-8. The car was wild, loud, hot. It would break your back, if you let it. It could do far worse.

It is possible to obtain a contemporary supercar that delivers that kind of raw driving experience, but it isn't clear why anyone would want to go that retro. With the GT40, of course, there was no choice. To see what it would be like to enjoy its nearly complete lack of obvious charms, just watch the 1966 film *A Man and a Woman*, directed by Claude Lelouch and starring Jean-Louis Trintignant as a French Le Mans driver who nearly dies at the wheel, prompting his wife's suicide. He stays with racing, becomes enamored of Anouk Aimée, and spends a scene testing a GT40 on the track. The true range of the car's ferocious nature is on display as it roars and whines through the steeply banked corners, while Trintignant takes the measure of its steering inside the deafening cockpit.

Nobody at Ford had any doubts that the GT supercar would be a runaway success. Drastically limiting production and setting the purchase price in the mid-$400,000 range would ensure that. The original GT40s had inspired a thriving replica market, with various period-appropriate V-8s dropped into the familiar chassis. The follow-up for the mid-2000s, which had sold for a mere $150,000, had achieved a cultish status. Sure, you could own a couple of Ferraris and a Lamborghini, maybe even something more exotic, like a Koenigsegg, Pagani, or Bugatti, but only a GT screamed "race car." It wasn't the car for millionaire wannabes. It was, and still is, the car for motoring enthusiasts with a deep sense of history. Henry Ford III wasn't breaking a sweat about whether there would be 500 applications for Ford GT ownership. He was probably worried that there would be 500,000.

The GT race car was an entirely different story. In the auto industry, a machine created for competition would ordinarily influence the design, technology, and engineering of sports cars intended for the driveway rather than the paddock. But there would be a logical sequence: racing would precede the road. The GT wasn't wasting time on that front. The supercar would be in many respects the same vehicle as the one assaulting the track in Florida and California in 2016 before heading to France. Parallel development made it a special player: it was really the only *true* purpose-built race car in the GTLM and GTE Pro fields in 2016.

While Multimatic's engineers were busting their asses to keep the car on schedule through 2014 and 2015, Ford was preparing for the GT's coming-out party. It wasn't a stressful process. In fact, it was the opposite.

"When we first went out for the first review of the GT clay models, our jaws dropped," Fields said. The executive team paid a visit to the Ford Product Development Center in Dearborn for the long-awaited moment. "I was stunned," he said, "at how quickly the teams worked and what they came back with."

And when the GT was revealed at the 2015 Detroit auto show, there was a collective intake of breath.

Not that it should have been such a surprise. After all, rumors about it had been circulating for at least a year. Still, the excitement just kept growing about Ford's storybook return to endurance racing in France to celebrate the fiftieth anniversary of the 1966 win. "This is a bigger deal than everyone expected," *Road & Track* magazine wrote in October 2014, a full three months before the GT blew everyone's doors off in Motown.

"Earthshaking" is how the magazine described the probability that a new Ford GT production car would be announced at the 2015 Detroit auto show. "Say it with me now," a scribe on the website *Jalopnik* wrote of the rumor: "Holy shitballs."

And then there it stood—a car that demanded a kind of reverent attention.

The new GT, in a brilliant "liquid blue" (Ford's new name for the color), rolled out onto a vast stage, over which a huge video screen flashed images of the new machine. Ford CEO Mark Fields presided over the reveal. "If you could use innovation to build the ultimate Ford performance vehicle," he said, "what would it be?"

He was then joined by Bill Ford for a few minutes of enticing banter.

"So, Bill, you think we ought to build it?" Fields asked.

"I think we should," the Ford scion replied, clearly relishing the historic moment.

"All right," Fields said. "How about we build it . . . hmmm. . . . How about next year?"

The crowd, as they say, went wild, because it knew *exactly* what that meant: a return to Le Mans.

It was a triumph for Ford, and it was also an early signal that 2015 was going to be the best year the U.S. auto industry had ever seen, a defiant comeback from the financial crisis.

When I saw the GT up close and in person at the New York auto show a few months later, I couldn't stop looking at it. The new car had advanced the art of the mid-engine supercar. Callum's swoopy, evocative design was defined by that pair of winglike flying buttresses at the car's rear. It was brash and bold, yet elegant and seductive, in the way Ferraris are. Callum's GT was beautiful, whereas the racing GT40s and the GTs of the mid-2000s were blunt. But the car was really more than beautiful. It was transcendent in its combination of the old and the new, in its blissful, enrapturing conjoining of the race car from the 1960s and state-of-the-art supercar from the twenty-first century. The reason it sent shock waves through the auto-enthusiast crowd and also blew away people who otherwise had little interest in cars was that it summarized, with a luminous visual presence, everything that a sports car was supposed to be. The GT looked sexy, technologically adventurous, very fast, very sleek, and very ready to race. Studying its lines and shapes was simultaneously relaxing—because everything was in the right place and in the right proportion—and thrilling. It was palpably dramatic, and it glowed from within. It was far from a big car, but it occupied physical space with an attitude of pure self-confidence. A lot of powerful, outlandish, expensive cars command attention, but the new GT was almost immediately respected. It didn't have to ask to join the club. It was already in.

The new GT established an entirely different tone in Detroit. The beast wasn't a reincarnation; it was a reinvention. *Wired* magazine called it "spectacularly ludicrous." "Holy mother of God," *Car and Driver* exclaimed. "We were floored." Mark Phelan of the *Detroit Free Press* wrote that it was "Stunningly gorgeous, remarkably advanced." Pulitzer Prize–winning car critic Dan Neil was enthusiastic about its "shattering, future-shock shape" in the *Wall Street Journal.*

The car *was* remarkable—and Ford had seized its moment. Who could know if it was now or never? By 2066, Le Mans could be the equivalent of a quaint nineteenth-century horse-jumping competition today. By 2066, we could be racing SpaceX Tesla hovercraft on the Mars colony. Or we could utter the words "auto racing" or "motorsport" and be greeted with blank stares from our robot overlords or our adult grandchildren, who consider car racing to be something that happened in an alarming percentage of early video games. The mid-twenty-first century's idea of a supercar could be a fully tricked-out Google pod-mobile that drives itself, converses about the symphonies of Beethoven and the more complicated corners of prime number theory, writes a little poetry when it's parked, and tops out at a bloodcurdling forty miles per hour.

The GT ultimately earned its considerable accolades as it was sent out on the car-show circuit. Over the course of 2015, it appeared in different liveries. The original blue car shown in Detroit was joined by a slick, metallic silver version. A yellow GT then came online. By the time the Detroit auto show reconvened in 2016, a new bright white GT was tucked away on a mezzanine display alongside the rest of the newly formed Ford Performance lineup: a Mustang, a Fiesta, even a pickup truck (the Raptor, a high-performance take on the F-150). The more colors the GT came in, the more captivating it became.

A few grouchy big-engine partisans took issue with the turbocharged V-6, even though 600 horsepower put the GT firmly in the same league as the newest Ferraris—and a cut above the stalwart 491-horsepower Corvettes that would be defending their 2015 Le Mans title.

By the beginning of the 2016 IMSA season, the Ford GT buzz was incandescent. Without question, this was the most anticipated racing debut in decades, trumping Formula One, NASCAR, and the Indianapolis 500. Best of all, Le Mans would represent the culmination of an entire racing *season*. Fans both experienced and new would be aware of the GT's performance, as it raced against its competition and sought to do something unprecedented: repeat history with a fresh new machine inspired by a fifty-year-old race car.

So, the Mustang wasn't transformed into a half-assed GTLM contestant. A clean-sheet design was green-lighted. There was no big risk that the cars wouldn't sell—Ford could already count the money. No, the challenge would be where it properly belonged: on the tracks leading up to that single, twenty-four-hour episode of exquisite torture in the French countryside.

Supercars are easy. Race cars are hard. The new GT had enjoyed a perfect birth. But it was now headed for its first major test.

Chapter 4 ═══════

Disaster at Daytona

For Ford, the lead-up to the Rolex 24 at Daytona in late January 2016 was a combination of pressure cooker and hype-a-palooza. Inside and outside the often-insular world of motorsports, everyone had become obsessed with the company's attempt to repeat history with the captivating and exceptionally sexy GT. That created steady external pressure, matched and exceeded by the internal pressure Ford put on itself.

Expectations seemed to outpace even what the carmaker had anticipated. Speculation about the company's return to endurance racing had been a constant thrum prior to the GT's reveal in Detroit in early 2015. After that, excitement picked up at a frantic pace, stoked by Ford as well as by fans and the media. Nobody was really calculating the odds, which said that a Le Mans win was a long shot after Ford's decades away from factory-supported endurance racing. The history that Ford was trying to repeat was also being overlooked: Ford may have won in 1966 but only after a dismal showing in 1964 and 1965.

Lurking behind all of this, of course, was the reality that Daytona would be the GT race car's first true test. In June, Ford had released a short video officially announcing what many had suspected: the GT would return to Le Mans. The film was thrilling and a bit out there. The Le Mans–winning car from the 1960s watches a grainy newsreel of itself and its legendary victory, then magically morphs into the new number 66 GT race car, fires up its engine, and blasts through the streets of Paris. En route to Le Mans, about two hours southwest of the French capital, the new GT frightens a rearing stallion, a *cavallino rampante*—throwing an obvious gauntlet down for Ferrari.

The imagery was exhilarating, the stuff of fanboy fantasies. But it also established a very high bar for Daytona.

And Daytona, when you talk about the cars hitting the track, is no pool party. This massive racing facility, located about two thirds of the way up the Florida peninsula, between Orlando and Jacksonville, is America's premier motorsports venue. It was the vision of Bill France, the patriarch of NASCAR, who dreamed of an epic venue for that unique creation of American racing, stock cars. Every February, it hosts the greatest NASCAR race of them all, the Daytona 500.

Constructed in 1959, the NASCAR track is a gigantic two-and-a-half-mile tri-oval, whose banking enables cars to achieve viciously high velocities. In qualifying, NASCAR competitors routinely top 200 miles per hour. The design of the banking allows physics to serve speed. As the cars slingshot around the turns, they are pressed down into the track rather than sliding off it.

Endurance racing is a completely different game from NASCAR competition, but it's also deeply wound into the Daytona DNA. Three major endurance races make up the so-called Triple Crown of this subset of motorsports, and Daytona is the only one besides Le Mans that goes for twenty-four hours (the third, Sebring, also in Florida, is a twelve-hour-long contest).

In fact, Daytona and Le Mans are the only twenty-four-hour races on the combined schedule of the North American IMSA

WeatherTech SportsCar Championship (sponsored by a company that makes expensive custom floor mats for cars and trucks) and the FIA World Endurance Championship in Europe.

Both Daytona and Le Mans run for a grueling full day, but they are distinguished by their courses. Le Mans is run over a combined road and racetrack course of eight and a half miles. Its most famous section, the fabled, terrifying Mulsanne Straight, is, at 3.7 miles, longer than the entire Daytona road course of 3.5 miles. It is why Le Mans is Le Mans. If you give a 600-horsepower GT car an uninterrupted expanse of nearly four miles to use as a drag strip, you are going to witness the type of velocity that freaks out most grown-ups. Put a 1,000-horsepower prototype car out there, and freaking out is no longer an option. The driver's eyes must stare ahead with a combination of professional precision and defiance of death—and trust that the car won't spin fatally out of control at some point.

A Ford engineer who worked on the original GT40 cars that captured the one-two-three victory expressed flat astonishment the first time he drove a normal road car around Le Mans's Circuit de la Sarthe, so named because it is located in the Sarthe *département*, which takes its name from the Sarthe River, a tributary of the Loire. He couldn't image how drivers would have the fortitude to push a car to 200 miles per hour on what was to him a long, two-lane county road, lined on either side by trees.

The Mulsanne isn't as hairy as it once was. In 1990, a pair of chicanes, or crimps, were added to the infamous straightaway, which the rest of the year is a public road, to get the drivers on their brakes before they hit speeds of 250 miles per hour. Two drivers, Jean-Louis Lafosse and Jo Gartner, had died in crashes in the 1980s. Gartner's car was shattered when it collided with a telephone pole. Lafosse's car was destroyed when it suffered a mechanical breakdown on the track and slid from one side to the other, guardrail to guardrail. Two race marshals were injured, and Lafosse's body was mutilated.

Daytona provides, in many respects, the next best (or worst) thing, in the form of those huge, arcing banks on the tri-oval, as well as a back straight that's broken by a quick, crisp bend known as the Bus Stop. It's here that drivers will try to make their lap times, taking a racing line through the turns that's as direct as possible.

Imagine you're required to attack this section of track over and over again, each time applying the sort of precise yet slightly imbalanced, edgy pressure that high-performance cars live for. Your machine, from tires to engine to gearbox, is at a limit. The once-glossy and colorful exterior is grimed with filth. You are sore and thirsty. You have stopped smelling anything but exhaust and racing fuel, and you can't remember a time when the scream of an engine created to evoke the battle cry of an angry animal wasn't filling your ears. It could be light. It could be dark. It could be raining. And still you must hit the Bus Stop and make your lap time, for an hour or more on each of your stints, until you hand the car over to one of your fellow drivers. Over the course of an entire day, by the clock, you and your codrivers could each be in the car for eight grueling hours, depending on the total duration of the race. "You've got to put down the laps," is what the drivers say.

In the back of your mind, you know that in endurance racing, deaths have come not because a driver pushed too hard, lost the grip and the car's rear, and drove straight into a wall, to perish in a 200-mile-per-hour fireball. Deaths in endurance racing have rather come because the driver drifted for a millisecond, lost that critical focus on the next moment of life, the next 100 feet of track, the consciousness that existence for a driver is defined not by the past, and not by any future that can be considered, but by a sort of barely extended present. You have no yesterday and you have no tomorrow. You have the next five seconds of *now*.

In endurance racing you know that, in this context, you also die because the car breaks. It's as if the horse is shot out from under you. One moment, you are as melded with a machine as you can be, wrestling the engine and the gearbox, the endlessly oversteering tires, but trusting in the bond. You're feeling good about life because this is, after all, what you've lived for since you slipped on a helmet for the first time and drove a go-cart, fast, at age ten. The next moment, part of your car explodes and shreds into bits of carbon fiber, alloy, and rubber, and you're looking for a place to crash or trying to use pure instinct to avoid killing your fellow racers.

Only once the initial trauma has subsided do you get to think about the imminent possibility of burning to death, assuming you're still alive and haven't lost an arm or a leg. Often, you can't even crawl from the wreckage. You have to be pulled. Bleeding. Dazed. Thankful.

Didier Theys, a Belgian who won Daytona twice, in 1998 and 2002, was the first real driver I ever met, and he acquainted me with the look I now associate with trained drivers—the gaze that out of habit is just slightly dislocated from the present, occupying instead a point in the future at the limit of vision. After all, at 140 miles per hour a driver is covering something like sixty-eight yards every second.

They say time travel is impossible, but professional drivers do it for a living. The increments are tiny, however. But they're repeated in a rhythm, like a pulse. This is what's simultaneously numbing and exhilarating about motorsport. The track itself is a defined experience, and the "racing line" is discovered relatively early in a race and scored with black tread marks from the abused tires. As a driver, you know where to go. But because you're going there so fast, you follow a simple rule: your hands on the steering wheel follow your eyes to the future.

This is a fundamental principle imparted by professional driving instructors. It sounds easy, but in practice it's extremely difficult. When driving, even on a track, we tend to manage a car in its current state. We feel the corner we're taking, or we deal with the second-by-second pace of acceleration. What we really need to be doing is borrowing the car's position from its future and creating a cognitive map, swiftly drawn, of the quickest trajectory to that position.

I've come to believe this can't really be taught, that drivers like Theys are born with an ability to process the present as contingent on a future that's just at the precipice of now. Because this doesn't drive them crazy, and they make a living from their talent, they can move through normal space and time. But when you look at the way they see, you can witness a kind of dislocation. Steve McQueen's character, Michael Delaney, put it best in *Le Mans*, the 1971 film whose objective was to capture the reality of motorsport with an emphatic, exceptional realism: "Racing's important to the men who do it well. When you're racing, it's life. Anything that happens before or after is just waiting."

When I met Theys he was retired, but this condition of waiting struck me as eternal. The air of anticipation was also permanent. He didn't exactly live in the now. He lived in the now immediately after the now, beheld with his handsome blue, piercing eyes. He could describe that imminent now in practical detail, because he would have to drive through it at 200 miles per hour and do it in one piece—again, and again, and again.

People like this are often just as quick with their humor as they are with their driving.

"What was your favorite race?" I asked Theys, knowing that he had run in three Indianapolis 500s and had finished third at Le Mans in 1999. The backdrop for this conversation was the raceway at Watkins Glen, in upstate New York, a big, fast track beloved by club racers and pros alike.

"The ones you win!" he exclaimed.

By its nature, Daytona is a study in contrasts, on two levels, when the Rolex 24 is being run.

First is the transformation of NASCAR's speed palace—and Daytona is surpassed only by Talladega, in Alabama, in velocity if not provenance—into a road course. NASCAR uses only the large track on the outside, the tri-oval, while the road race combines that with the winding course that sits on the infield. And it's not just the racing layout that changes. For the weekend of the Rolex 24, this redneck Elysium just off one of Florida's less fashionable stretches of beachfront attracts the moneyed, middle-aged aristocracy that favors endurance racing in America. (Things are far more egalitarian in Europe, as I would learn six months later at Le Mans.) The Daytona 500 features hulking stock cars, while the Rolex 24 showcases out-there prototypes and sleek GT cars. The only connecting threads in 2016 were the Corvette team, which included GT racers that share a corporate stable with the Chevys that run in the Daytona 500; and Ford, which had a similar NASCAR link. Otherwise, the Rolex 24 is Porsches, Audis, Aston Martins, and of course Ferraris.

And the Ferrari presence is one that defines how different sports-car racing is from the snarling hoedown that is NASCAR.

Other manufacturers and teams provide amenities for their fans and competitors during the Daytona marathon. But Ferrari has a raised red-and-white temple overlooking the track's first turn, at the end of a patio section attached to the pits. Several thousand square feet of viewing platforms, enclosed and both heated and air-conditioned, are filled with Ferraristas for the duration of the race, most of them decked out in Ferrari-logo attire and attended to by a staff of waitresses and bartenders who are participating in their own marathon of hospitality. They'll keep at it for the full twenty-four hours, even though all but the most die-hard supporters of Maranello, Italy's most famous enterprise, will retire after nightfall to nearby hotels.

In a month, the speedway will be turned over to the rollicking, proudly redneck bacchanal that is the Daytona 500. But for the twenty-four-hour race, in addition to the impressive Ferrari presence, there's also an abundance of Rolex. The watchmaker, founded in the early twentieth century, sells the world's most widely coveted luxury timepieces. Indeed, there are finer watches that you can strap on your wrist—Patek Philippe, Vacheron Constantin, Audemars Piguet—but Rolex has heft and the wherewithal to sponsor motorsport. It also has the investment-grade status. A Rolex is money in the bank, backed by credibility in the paddock. In this respect, it's rivaled only by TAG Heuer, with its longtime Formula One association.

The country-club atmosphere at Daytona for the endurance race is the ideal environment for Rolex, and the Swiss firm knows it. Enormous green and gold signage rules the speedway, creating a branded vibe amid the roar and thrust, the sonic dissonance, that's as soothing as what one might encounter at another sporting event synonymous with Rolex and class: the Wimbledon tennis tournament in England.

The Rolex 24 winners enjoy perhaps the best reward in the world of speedway competition. The members of each team to win its division are given a Rolex Daytona chronograph, probably the sexiest timepiece on the planet these days. Rolex is legendary for such automatic timepieces as the Submariner divers' watch and the Datejust, a dress watch favored by several U.S. presidents, but for some time now its most collectible watch has been the Daytona, named for the speedway and the endurance race. It was famously worn by Paul Newman, a semipro racer, and Daytonas that evoke the timekeeping tool Newman favored for his talented wrist, from the proper vintage, bring in the most money of any contemporary Rolexes at auctions. A new Daytona will run you $15,000. Some drivers at the Rolex 24 own several. One driver has seven; he wears the piece from his first win and has distributed the rest to friends and family. Chip Ganassi wears a gold and stainless-steel model.

The funny thing about the drivers at the Rolex 24 is that although many have run in other racing categories, driving vehicles ranging from open-wheel Indy cars to snarling NASCAR beasts, most perceive how prestigious the Daytona race is and what a cosmopolitan contrast endurance racing in general presents to more provincial brands of competition.

"NASCAR is Walmart," Scott Atherton, the president of IMSA, told me. "And I mean that in the most admiring way. But sports-car racing is Nordstrom."

In after-race interviews, for example, you can tell that the guys who won watches are psyched, while the ones who didn't are, well, disappointed, like kids who missed out on a primo toy at Christmas. This prestige is one of the more distinctive elements of the Rolex 24. It reminds you that endurance racing, with Le Mans as the crown jewel, has lodged itself in the collective aspirations of professional drivers everywhere; only Formula One and the Indy 500 carry the same cognitive heft.

Not that glistening stainless-steel Swiss chronographs, Ferrari's ad hoc spectators' Parthenon, Ford's own hospitality party just a few hundred feet away, and a steady parade of handsome, risk-taking drivers can overcome the blood, sweat, grime, smoke, and sometimes even fire that define the Rolex 24 race itself. A driver can spend a couple of hours in the car, or he could be in it for fourteen, depending on how his team parcels out the stints. (Although total drive time is capped, the IMSA rules are more focused on ensuring that a driver spends a *minimum* amount of time behind the wheel in a stint, typically about an hour.) Each car that finishes, of course, stays on the track for the duration, limited only by the amount of fuel it can take on—each team is given a defined amount of fuel that has to last for the whole race—and the necessity of replacing mechanical components, such as brakes, or switching tires. The racing authorities' rules aim to bring the cars from each team into some kind of competitive parity. Fuel capacity for each type of car, for example, is controlled so that in a given class all the competitors will be able to turn the same number of laps before refueling—more or less, because a driver can always push his luck.

There's a classical dimension to endurance racing. Remember that the first marathon, run in ancient Greece in 490 BC, when the Greek messenger Pheidippides brought Athens news of a victory over the Persians at the Battle of Marathon, was undertaken not for athletic glory but to inform a civilization that it wouldn't be conquered. The runner's journey ended right before his own death, with a single word, "victory."

Endurance racing, at a vital strategic level, is all about breaking your competitors' cars and, by association, their will. But at its *base* level, a race like Daytona presents a simple racing objective: complete as many official laps as possible in the time frame of the event. But we're not talking about flipping on the cars and letting them run. An endurance race is an improvisational undertaking. As in warfare, no battle plan survives first contact with the enemy.

The best place to take this in at the speedway is from pit lane, long after night has fallen, when the cars have been running for over twelve hours. Everyone's soul is tested during this treacherous period. This is when mistakes, big mistakes, are made, after the fans have dropped off to sleep in the RVs in the infield or, if well heeled, have headed back to hotels by the beach.

The drivers, racing teams' majordomos, and most important, the pit and garage crews get few breaks. Sure, off their stints the drivers can duck into their own rock-star-style RVs for a shower, food, some shut-eye. But the crews go all day and all night and into the next day. If you ask, most drivers will tell you that at the twenty-four-hour races in particular, it's hard to sleep and tough to eat properly. Many drivers concentrate on staying hydrated, because drinking fluids is easy. And they have to be constantly prepared to jump back into the car.

The images from pit lane are, for the uninitiated, borderline hellish. Shattered things are everywhere, space is tight, and the endless drone of engines being pushed to their limit is oppressive. You wear earplugs or sound-canceling headphones when you wander amid the carnage and dodge the carts and negotiate the narrow lane behind the pits that holds loads of fresh tires.

You watch your step, because there are hoses everywhere. You stay out of the way. You could be grievously injured: pit crashes aren't unheard of, and the crews wear full fire-protection suits and racing helmets for a reason. The explosive wail of a 600-horsepower engine being revved as a car drops off its hydraulic jacks after receiving four new tires and a fresh tank of fuel is enough to make your eardrums detonate and spurt blood. The first time I ever experienced this—stupidly, without earplugs—I thought I'd never be able to listen to music again. I pictured future conversations with my kids punctuated by an elderly, *"Huh?"*

A car race takes arena rock and turns it up well beyond eleven. And although it is noise, not music, it creates a kind of crude symphony that does something music can't do. It grabs you in the gut. Pete Townshend of The Who—who had his hearing obliterated in the 1970s by the violent decibels of gigantic Marshall amplifier stacks—wasn't going to windmill his arm off against the strings of his guitar. But a GTLM car, despite its multitude of safety features, when out of control *could* shred a person and then incinerate what was left. Drivers know this. In motorsport the possibility of death—horrible, mutilating death—is a given. Doctors who have examined killed racers have expressed grim wonder at how the human body could be so gruesomely traumatized.

In the hours just before dawn, everything starts to break: machinery, bodies, the will to go on. Much like soldiers at war, the drivers and crew have to fall back on their training. The adrenaline rush takes you only so far. Sixteen hours into the race, beat drivers are sleeping where they fall, some using stacks of tires as rude mattresses and pillows. They don't shed the fireproof racing suits; they don't even lose the helmets. The ones who are awake steal smoke breaks far from the fuel canisters. It will probably take two or three showers to wash off the race and a week or more to physically recover from an entire day in the pit-lane trenches.

The work of fixing what's broken never ends. During one of my late-night strolls through pit lane, I saw two guys devoutly focused on using a blowtorch to rid a tire of debris it had picked up on the racetrack. Blobs of molten rubber had dried on the tarmac, forming a morass of black shapes. Cars that had utterly failed were wheeled back to the paddock by packs of men bent in concern and humiliation; the cars then disappeared into a garishly lit repair bay to be ripped apart by mechanics.

But even in this stygian context, the pride of profession is evident. Another crew member polished the filth from wheels. At least a small part of the car should look shiny and new. Amid the marathon of insanity, while the roaring peloton of cars made its way around the track, again and again, professionalism was never forgotten. Everyone here does this for a living.

On the brilliantly sunny start day of the Rolex 24 in January 2016, the Ford GTs attracted more attention prerace, when the fans get to mass onto the track for a walk-around, than anything else in competition. With their pleasing angles and new red-white-and-blue racing livery, the GTs stood out, even alongside the exotic prototype cars.

The motorsports world had been salivating for months. The website *Sportscar365* called the upcoming racing season "a five-way factory fight between Porsche, Corvette, BMW, Ferrari and newcomers Ford," heralding "a potential new golden age for GT racing in North America."

"The GT Le Mans category has been the most competitive, most intriguing category I've been in, in the last seven, eight, nine years," BMW Team RLL co-owner Bobby Rahal told the publication.

And Ford was ready. Or *thought* it was ready, after months of testing, of taking the prototype GTs and making them into track-ready race cars. There had been few problems, and the verdict from the drivers was that the GT was fantastic. Even the funkier elements of the new turbo V-6 EcoBoost—the blats and burps and whirs that had struck some early obsessives watching guerrilla video of testing on YouTube—seemed to be winning everyone over as the engine was tuned.

"We don't want to be overconfident," said Raj Nair, Ford's chief technical officer and overseer of both this new GT program and the previous generation from the mid-2000s, in a video Ford posted online.

"We're almost kind of worried about how good it's going," he added. That would turn out to be an ominous statement.

The race started at precisely 2:40 p.m., but the lead-up consumed the entire morning and early afternoon, as fans were given the chance to walk the starting grid, check out the cars, and meet the drivers in person. The Ford GTs were the undisputed stars of the show, but the yellow Corvettes and red Ferraris drew their share of attention. Under the calm winter sun of central Florida, the machines glistened, pristine in their prerace preparation. By roughly this time tomorrow, they'd be encrusted with tire fragments sucked up from the track. Some would be gouged and dented from battle. A few would have their carbon-fiber fronts and flanks shredded by collisions with walls and other cars.

Half of Ford's team and half of its race cars were on hand. (The rest were preparing for the FIA World Endurance Championship in Europe.) Like the cars, the drivers looked luminous in their racing suits. One thing almost everyone notices about pro drivers right away is they aren't big guys. Some are tall, but none are *really* tall. And most are wiry and short, five foot six, five seven, five eight. This is self-selection and the Darwinism of racing. Big dudes don't fit in the cars, and they add weight.

Joey Hand, thirty-six at the time, was in the number 66 car. I got to know him a bit during the season and had grown accustomed to his bent nose, which reminded me of the poet Frank O'Hara's. But Hand has no poetic brooding in him; he's a driver who's cool and cheerful when not in the seat. He was joined in the 66 car by forty-year-old German driver Dirk Müller, a Le Mans veteran who won at Daytona in 2011 when racing for BMW; and Sébastien Bourdais, a bespectacled Frenchman, like Hand thirty-six years old, with half a dozen Indy 500s and three second-place Le Mans results in the top prototype class with Peugeot.

Thirty-four-year-old Australian Ryan Briscoe and forty-year-old Englishman Richard Westbrook were in the number 67 car, as was thirty-four-year-old German driver Stefan Mücke. Briscoe had come over to Ganassi's team after a win at Daytona with Corvette Racing in 2015. Westbrook had run Daytona and Le Mans numerous times with Corvette, and joined Briscoe in defecting from the General Motors factory team to the new Ford factory team. Mücke's last four runs at Le Mans in a GT car had been with Aston Martin.

All these GT drivers were in the Platinum category, the highest designation in competitive racing, and within each car they'd split the driving between them more or less equally.

In the pits, Chip Ganassi paced inside the Ford Performance tent, while his guys monitored data on screens and stayed on the radio with the drivers. It took me almost the entire spring and early summer racing seasons to nail Ganassi down long enough to chat about the pressure, but when we got our chance, he came through.

Ganassi is a native of Pittsburgh, still lives there, and has that taciturn steelworkers' town in his blood. He has a reputation for chewing up journalists and spitting them out. He's solidly built, even a bit paunchy, and his default expression is flinty. After fooling around with motorcycle racing, he started driving race cars professionally in his late teens and had some good results in his five outings at the Indy 500, including an eighth-place finish in 1983. A wreck a year later would send him into retirement, however, and into what in retrospect is clearly his true calling: founder, owner, and CEO of Chip Ganassi Racing.

In that role he's raced in the IndyCar Series and captured four Indy 500 victories. He has also run in NASCAR, in addition to endurance racing. In person, he alternates between a calculating taciturnity and what might best be described as sudden jollity. Ganassi has figured out, it seems, all the moving parts of what it takes to be a successful racing-team owner. And there are many moving parts. But even he was taken aback by what he'd gotten himself into with the Ford Le Mans campaign.

"I had no idea the amount of passion that this program stirred in people," he told me. "A lot of people remember the Ferrari-Ford battle. But I gotta be honest, if Ford had come back to Le Mans with a car that had a different shape to it, I don't think it would be as interesting." Then he laughed, loudly and freely.

"If they'd come back with something different—oh, I don't know, a *Mustang* or something—I don't think it would be as exciting! Call me crazy, but that's what I think."

This is how Chip Ganassi deals with his anxiety. He brings out his secretly wicked sense of humor, which combines with the pressures of the moment to reveal small truths, along with what he thinks about those truths. Talking to him, I was reminded of a great poker player, who stares you down through bet after bet on a big pot, with the chips piling up, never much changing that expression, making you think there's nothing going on in that head, no possibility of a bluff.

And then when he has you, when you abruptly realize he had held the good cards all along and was just reeling you in, free of emotion, he cuts loose with the broad smile and the big guffaws as he throws down his winning hand and rakes in your chips. Thanks for playing the game, kid. Thanks for playing *my* game.

At Daytona, Ganassi's big issue with the GTs had nothing to do with the cars. The problem was that he hadn't been able to assert his usual control over the effort, and that this caused some chafing. He probably expected it, given the scale of Ford's ambition. But he didn't like it.

Henry Ford III, only thirty-three, hung back behind the racing professionals, expressionless but probably nervous as hell. Yet the burden of Ford's 1966 achievement really wasn't on him alone—the road to Le Mans was far more than a one-man show this time around.

The Audi R8 safety car led the field around for a few laps, the green flag was waved, and they were off. The 2016 IMSA Weather-Tech SportsCar Championship had begun.

The GTs came out with guns blazing. Both the number 66 car, with Hand at the wheel, and the number 67, driven by Briscoe, turned fast laps. In short order, they were in the lead pack. But just as Ford fans were settling into that situation, disaster struck—not after hours of racing, but right away.

Briscoe's number 67 car developed a gearbox problem—it was slipping from fifth to sixth gear. In his 2016 debut with Ganassi, in the hottest ride to hit endurance racing in a decade, Briscoe found himself unable to downshift after only about twenty-five laps. This meant he had no power when he needed it, to get out of the corners or to take it to the straights. For an agonizing half hour, the car sat on pit lane. But it couldn't be repaired there and had to be pushed back to the garage.

Henry Ford III looked on pensively, a tinge of concern playing across his features, but he continued to greet reporters warmly. Ganassi, by contrast, was grim-faced. He had lots of work to do on the track. Not only was his organization handling the GTs, now in crisis, but he also had a car in the next class up, the so-called prototypes. That car would be his last in that dance, which he had already won six times at Daytona, most recently in 2015. He wouldn't be back in that class in 2017. So he wanted to go out with a bang, repeating victory in 2016. That meant he had to manage the GT situation, while also keeping one eye on the prototype race happening on the track at the same time.

But the number 66 GT was performing well for the moment, in the afternoon sunshine. While Briscoe and 67 were out, number 66, driven by Joey Hand, surged into second place in the GTLM class, dueling with Ferrari.

Once the 67 car was in the garage, it became clear that it wouldn't be returning to the race anytime soon. The problem was going to take a while to fix. Briscoe and his teammates had to wait it out.

The fact was that the 67 car had been having problems all week, through the qualifying rounds. In the garage, the rear spoiler was pulled off and a hulking crew member knelt on the massive carbon-fiber diffuser, before that too was removed. Replacement parts were hauled in. The tires came off, and the process of dismantling the entire rear end commenced.

The car had looked glorious just a few hours earlier, sleek and powerful, like a superhero. Now, it resembled a crippled combatant being treated at a field hospital.

Gearbox failures are vexing but not uncommon in endurance racing, where gears are being constantly and harshly shifted under extreme stress. The GTs' gearshifts, in fact, had been a source of preoccupation for fans who had watched the car undergoing testing on YouTube videos for months before Daytona. The sound was like a sledgehammer striking an anvil, and when it was joined by that of the belching turbocharged V-6 engine, it caused fans' heads to spin. "The New Ford GT on Track Sounds Violently Sick" was a *Jalopnik* headline after the videos aired.

An agonizing forty-five minutes after the failure, Briscoe was running again in the 67 car, but he was in fifty-third place overall, and he had an impossible amount of ground to make up over the next twenty-three hours. Unfortunately, the number 66 car was also in trouble. Hand's car pitted at lap forty-two, and while the crew was undertaking a usually routine brake replacement—a process that should take only about two minutes—a brake line was damaged. The video feeds showed brake fluid dribbling onto pit lane, leaking like urine. It was a pathetic sight, and it ultimately put the 66 car well back on laps as well—and that was before it, too, had a gearbox failure and had to be pushed back to the paddock bays.

The 66 came back out with twenty hours to go, but though the race had really barely begun, the lap deficit for the GTs was already insurmountable. Both were running dead last in the GTLM class. Sure, they were fast, but they weren't durable, and the combination of durable and fast is what wins the Rolex 24. Through the night and into the next day, Ganassi's drivers turned fast lap after fast lap, slowly chewing their way up the standings, passing slower cars in the next class down and hoping that a few Porsches, BMWs, and Ferraris would hit their own patches of trouble—which, as it turns out, they did.

The Corvettes, on the other hand, were tanks. By the last half hour of the race, both cars and their drivers were given permission to go full out, and the finish was close, a drag race, with one Vette winning by a nose.

It was Ford versus Chevy versus Ferrari, old rivals taking one another on at the debut and the pinnacle of the U.S. endurance-racing season. On paper it sounded fantastic. But on the track, Daytona was a grueling disappointment for Ford—a monumental emotional blow. The numbers 66 and 67 GTs finished seventh and ninth in their class, respectively.

A week after the Daytona catastrophe, there was still plenty of postgame chatter about the GTs that had both spent so much precious time in the garage instead of turning lead laps on the track.

Two basic views emerged. One held that the cars' struggles were to be expected. Sure, we'd seen the GT taking test laps, and while the turbocharged six-cylinder sounded pretty nasty at times, the car hadn't looked as if it were going to break down.

Nor did Ford Performance suggest that there were any looming problems. At the Detroit auto show, just weeks before the GTs' Daytona debut at the Rolex 24, Ford Performance's boss, Dave

Pericak, put any naysayers' questions to rest, decisively: "We are ready to race," he declared.

But Chip Ganassi was grumbling. There were too many cooks in the kitchen for his taste, too many points of view on the car. This was a marquee effort, and his struggle at the head of the racing team was to square what had to happen on and off the track with the rapidly building media frenzy around the GT and Ford's return to Le Mans. Adding to Ganassi's problems was his management of two semi-independent racing teams on opposite sides of the Atlantic.

He later confessed that he had worried about all this before Daytona and that his nightmares had come true. The highly accelerated timetable for getting the GT racing, in the United States and Europe, had been grating on him. But he was dealing with it. That's what you do when you run the second-most-successful racing organization in history. You deal with the bullshit and move on.

By any reckoning, the Rolex 24 was going to be a tough start for the car. Yes, the GT had been bred for the track, with the race car and the road car developed simultaneously. The GT had thoroughbred written all over it—it looked shockingly more ferocious than anything else in the GTLM class, including the privateer Dodge Vipers and the new Ferrari 488s. It certainly struck anyone with eyes as more race car than the Corvettes that had been dominating the class. Compared with the GTs, the bright yellow Vettes were almost like NASCAR machines; a huge, supercharged V-8 sat under the hood, but the Vettes' drivers and crews had to compensate for all that oomph and weight up front. Still, the Corvettes had shown that they were both pretty fast and superlatively reliable. What they lacked in flamboyance and daring design, they more than made up for with their solid nature. Simply put, they didn't break.

Fans of the GT also noted that when the cars were running free of trouble, they ran very, very fast. Raw speed in a straight line and quickness into the corners equaled a perfect endurance-racing car—as long as the durability actually came through. In fact, how fast the GTs could consistently go would create a minor controversy and some grumbling during the season, especially in Europe—and that grumbling would burst into public view just one day before Le Mans.

The other view that emerged after Daytona was the argument that the car wasn't ready for prime time, and that Ford had been served a bit of karmic comeuppance, after promoting its return to endurance racing quite avidly for a year. The mutterings I heard around the car-show circuit prior to the Rolex 24 suggested that Ford was not in for an easy time; even though Ferrari wasn't running a factory team, it was debuting its own mid-engine sports car, and the drivers working for the privateer outfits were some of the best in the business.

"They're going to bleed red"—that was how Ferrari's drivers would approach the lead-up to Le Mans and their somewhat involuntary role as the foils to Ford's efforts to revisit upon Ferrari the humiliation of 1966.

As it turned out, Ferrari just missed out on a third-place finish at Daytona. The 488s were quick, but they couldn't hang with the Corvettes on the huge, banked curves and straightaways of the NASCAR sections of the track, where the Vettes' power plants found drag-racing heaven. The in-car video feeds told the story, as the TV and radio commentators were happy to remind anyone tuned in over the course of the twenty-four hours. "Just listen to the sound of a big American V-8 at full, growling, heavy-metal song," one said.

The GTs, meanwhile—those very pretty, very technologically advanced GTs, custom-sculpted from carbon fiber by Multimatic—had languished in the Ganassi garage, their carefully crafted red-white-and-blue body panels scattered around the cars as mechanics dug into the internals and engineers looked on with consternation and concern.

I wasn't surprised the GTs had problems. Practice is practice, and racing is racing. It's a truism in motorsports, especially apt in endurance racing, where the format is intended to break the cars. One of the Porsche 911s at Daytona, after running impeccably for over twenty hours, basically exploded. It was pushed back to the garage to finish out the race in a widening puddle of engine oil oozing from its destroyed flat-six.

The GT was without question a fast car. It goes without saying that racing requires fast. The Vettes had it flat out. The Ferraris had it in the twisty parts. But the GTs had it everywhere. And they weren't *that* much slower than the 1,000-horsepower prototypes they shared the Daytona course with. In fact, one of the two GTs posted the fastest GTLM lap time for the entire race, and both cars turned some of the fastest laps on the track as they fought to catch up from their deep deficits. But the 1965 GTs were fast cars, too. The reliability, however, was up for debate; the GTs that had taken on Le Mans that year were all retired.

Would the story of the GT end with an epic victory, as in 1966? Or was Daytona a bad omen?

Dave Pericak had thought the GTs were ready to race. A twenty-two-year veteran of Ford, Pericak wasn't a guy to make light-hearted declarations that he intended to twist around later when they didn't pan out. He was all business, all the time, although he was also quick to grin, and his determination never seemed to cause him misery. Ford had given him responsibility for probably its most important vehicle, the Mustang, and had asked him to oversee as chief engineer the creation of a new model for 2015.

"Dave did a great job with Mustang," Mark Fields told me. "So we put him in charge of Ford Performance."

No big deal, right? His job before had been to not screw up the most famous sports car Ford had ever created, and now he was being asked to not screw up one of the biggest returns to racing in the history of the sport. And not only the CEO was watching; the entire Ford family was, as well.

A compact, intense man, Pericak shares with professional racers that ability to peer deeply into the future, to imagine not just the next curve but the endless deluge of them that makes up an endurance race that starts in daylight, runs through the darkness, and concludes long after the sun has risen.

"We were very happy with how the car performed," Pericak told me. "But we were very disappointed with its durability."

He admitted that the entire return to Le Mans to celebrate the fiftieth anniversary of the win was run "at light speed," and he showed plenty of humility when he said he wished the program had had more time. But I heard the frustration in his voice—the sense that Ford Performance and Multimatic had let down the drivers and the company.

"I take everything personally," Pericak said, holding back on throwing blame around. "The way the cars struggled tore me apart inside, but I don't let it get me down. Outwardly, there's not a bigger cheerleader for the team than me."

The critical failure with the number 66 and 67 cars turned out to be minor and race-day fluky: a small actuator had failed. But Pericak pointed out that it was actually *better* for the GTs to share a fault than to have separate ones. Different problems would double the troubleshooting. A bad gearbox could be fixed, and without forcing a switch in transmission suppliers, in the four GTs that would, as Pericak said, in a return to his brand of straightforward, borderline-cocky language, "stage an assault on Le Mans."

But his confidence wasn't being restored without some shame. Ford had been promoting the GT and its return to racing for a year.

The drivers were among the best in the business, on both sides of the Atlantic. Chip Ganassi Racing knew what it was doing. For months, the drivers had been praising the car. They were ready to go. But almost immediately, the GT wasn't.

"I told Chip and the team that they had done an amazing job," Pericak said. The next part came without a beat. "But we owe them a durable race car." The next part came even faster. "There's never been a car more born to race than this one. And we all have skin in the game."

But nobody from Ford left Daytona either soaked in Champagne or sporting a new Rolex watch.

The game would now move on to the 12 Hours of Sebring in March. For Pericak, for Ganassi, for the Ford brass, and for the GTs, the pressure would be cranked up about as high as it could go. After all, they were out to repeat history.

PART II

ALL RIGHT, WE'LL BEAT HIS ASS

Chapter 5

Ford Would Like to Buy Ferrari

In the mid-1960s, Henry Ford II and Enzo Ferrari decided they couldn't stand each other.

It was a completely different era in the auto industry, long before the gas crisis of the 1970s and the arrival of Japanese and German brands in the U.S. market. The Detroit Big Three ruled America, and there was even room for a fourth player, American Motors Corporation (AMC), run by George Romney, who would go on to be governor of Michigan (and whose son, Mitt, would be Massachusetts governor and a two-time presidential candidate). In the 1950s, the elder Romney's claim to fame was overseeing the rollout of the AMC Rambler, a relatively small car by the standards of a decade known for excessive chrome and flamboyant tail fins on cars whose front ends seemed to arrive five minutes before their rears.

The Rambler was called the "dinosaur fighter," and it presaged the battle the prehistoric Big Three would fight in the 1970s. (AMC would become even more famous during that decade when it acquired the World War II Jeep brand from Kaiser, another U.S.

automaker operating in the shadow of the Big Three; Jeep would later become Chrysler's most important brand, after AMC was absorbed in 1987.)

Imports, in those days, were from Europe. The Volkswagen Beetle had arrived in 1949 as a one-off import. VW would set up shop in the United States in 1955, and the car really took off in the 1960s. Like the Rambler, the Beetle was a counterpoint to the enormous sedans the Big Three were selling.

But the Beetle wasn't a sports car, and that's what the Big Three thought of when they thought about Europe. As BMW wouldn't introduce the sports sedan to America until the late 1960s, the nameplates consisted mainly of one German, one Brit, and two, possibly three, Italians. Porsche. Jaguar. Ferrari. Lamborghini.

Alfa Romeo could also be counted, and its Spider roadster gained fame in the 1967 countercultural coming-of-age film *The Graduate*, from the director Mike Nichols. The MGB roadster from the British Motor Corporation was also a somewhat familiar sight. But the roadsters were for bohemian rakes and sophisticated college kids. The real sports cars were creatures of the racetrack.

And the men who ran America's auto industry knew it. These marques were different from what was common on both U.S. roads and U.S. racetracks. Racing was controversial in the United States at this time, anyway. In the 1950s, concerned that racing was encouraging reckless behavior both on and off the track, the American Automobile Manufacturers Association called for a ban on carmakers' participation in or support of motorsports. The Big Three went along with the ban, from 1957 until Ford broke the ban in 1962.

What intrigued people about the European sports cars was the usual mixture of features that woo straightforward, plainspoken Yanks to the charms of the Old World: sexiness, chiefly, but also a spirited attitude toward driving and an embrace of timeless beauty over the notion that cars are A-to-B machines. Sure, Detroit had lost its mind in the 1950s and created some of the most out-there, exuberant, overdone cars of all time, orgies of thrusting hood ornaments, dramatic tail fins, thick whitewall tires, wild colors, and oceans of chrome. But by the 1960s that excess had all been dialed back. Ford's "pony car," the Mustang, would be introduced in 1964, following the Chevrolet Corvette roadster by a decade, and the brutalist muscle cars that would define the brawny side of Detroit would arrive over the next ten years.

The really stylish stuff, either dripping with sex in the case of the Italians, oozing panache like the Jags and Aston Martins, or proposing the perfect driving experience, à la Porsche, was a European thing. And the racing added a dash of danger to the seductiveness.

When Henry Ford II—nicknamed "the Deuce"—thought about what he really wanted in life, he wanted some of that sex and style. The son of Edsel Ford and grandson of Henry Ford, the Deuce was a man of considerable appetites and ambitions. He had a taste for European cars and European women, and he wasn't reluctant to act on his urges. In 1965, he left his wife and married his Italian mistress, Maria Cristina Vettore Austin, who would appear on the cover of *Life* magazine in a Detroit Lions T-shirt.

But Cristina ultimately didn't represent his boldest Italian conquest. Henry Ford II wanted to buy Ferrari. And he almost did.

Henry Ford II was actually the perfect American to make a play for the Italian carmaker. The Deuce was one of those mid-century scions of industry who combined worldly self-confidence with a well-tailored masculine swagger and a passion for business. He was no entitled layabout, happy to live off his inherited lucre while savoring the 1950s' and 1960s' never-ending, sun-chasing party for wealthy elites. There could have been frequent touchdowns in New York, London, Rome, Paris, Hollywood, the south of France, Monaco, the Italian islands, and before the Cuban Revolution,

Havana. He had the wherewithal and could be indulged—being a Ford has never automatically meant following in the founder's giant footsteps. Working in the family business is optional and at times has been actively discouraged, given that certain heirs have lacked the competence to manage a global manufacturing enterprise.

Henry Ford II's grand and often grandiose life has been thoroughly examined, investigated, and recounted, but the short version is that in 1945, when he wasn't yet thirty years old, he took charge of Ford on his father's death and dragged the original American car company, an icon of the second industrial revolution, into the modern business world. He did so by making two critical decisions.

First, he brought in a group of number crunchers from the Army Air Forces. They hadn't beaten the Nazis and the Japanese militarists all by themselves. But they had proved that victory in war, and later success in business, could be ruthlessly quantified and statistically scrutinized. The Whiz Kids, as they were called, took Ford out of its play-by-feel, postwar mode and into the new age of management by hard data. One of them, Robert McNamara, would become president of Ford in 1960 and later John F. Kennedy's and then Lyndon Johnson's secretary of defense, presiding over the early phases of the Vietnam War.

Second, Henry Ford II believed that employee Lee Iacocca was onto something with a new car called the Mustang. Henry II had put Iacocca in charge of the Ford division of the Ford Motor Company (like General Motors, Ford was a holding company, encompassing Ford, Lincoln, Mercury, and Ford Credit, which had been set up in the late 1950s, despite Henry Ford's distaste for lending at interest).

The company has on balance enjoyed more successful runs with other vehicles, namely the F-Series pickup truck. But Iacocca's Mustang (in truth, he wasn't the only Ford executive or employee to champion the first 'Stang, but he was an instrumental mover and shaker) is Ford's most iconic car except for the Model T, which naturally is no longer in production. The only other Ford vehicle ever built that has inspired such raptures of loyalty and enthusiasm as the Mustang is, of course, the Le Mans–winning GT40.

But we'll get to that car shortly, and for what it's worth, almost no GT40s made it to the road, while Mustangs have hit the highways in the United States by the millions—and more recently have become the most popular sports cars in Europe.

Iacocca's insight was simplicity itself: young people want a young people's car. When he took Henry II up on his offer to run the Ford division, he saw a wave of people under thirty hitting the U.S. car market. They weren't going to buy a hulking sedan—they were going to want something fun.

This was what Henry II saw in Iacocca—not a gasoline-in-the-veins gearhead, not a number cruncher like McNamara, but a *salesman*. If Iacocca thought there was a market that was about to be underserved by Ford's products, then Iacocca was probably right. The guy was born to sell. Let him create something that he could sell, and you were home free.

It's all more complicated than the Whiz Kids and the Mustang, but those two developments nonetheless nicely capture what made Henry Ford II a great leader. There was a third idea, however. It wasn't critical to Ford's business, but it would set the company on a trajectory that would conclude in France in June 1966.

Enzo Ferrari was a dirt-poor working-class Italian kid who fell in love with racing the first time he saw a Fiat running flat out. He became a driver for Fiat, and later for Alfa Romeo, and in 1929 he founded the Scuderia Ferrari, which was intended to build race cars for Alfa. After the war, the Scuderia (which means "stable" in

Italian) would build race cars for itself, and its first big win would come at the 24 Hours of Le Mans of 1949. One of the winning car's drivers was Luigi Chinetti, an exceptionally important individual in Ferrari's history; it was he who would start selling Ferraris in America and open a vast U.S. auto market to the road-car arm of the Scuderia that Enzo would establish in 1947, entirely to fund his racing efforts.

The company, even today, begins and ends with the Scuderia, even though its road cars have been with us for decades and have graced, in poster form, the bedroom walls of countless young men. Maybe Ferrari fans don't yearn to race so much as they yearn for everything the brand represents: speed, sexy red cars, and lots of money. Ferraris pop up everywhere in the culture: on television in *Magnum, P.I.* (a 308 GTB) and *Miami Vice* (a Daytona) and in movies such as *Ferris Bueller's Day Off* (a replica 1961 250 GT California Spyder) and *National Lampoon's Vacation* (another 308, possibly outclassed by its driver, the leggy blond model and actress Christie Brinkley).

What really matters to the company, however, is racing, and for much of Ferrari's history, racing meant Le Mans and Formula One. It was the perfect one-two punch. Formula One was the acid test of speed, performance, technology, and driver skill, and Ferrari has never missed a season since the modern form of the racing series was developed in the postwar period. Le Mans wins would prove reliability and validate various types of technology developed for the prolonged speeds and changing conditions of the Circuit de la Sarthe, while the race itself would stress long-term strategy and teamwork.

Racing is expensive, and unlike Ford and General Motors in the United States, carmakers that were rediscovering factory-supported racing with stock cars in the 1960s, Ferrari wasn't selling millions of cars and trucks a year to a gigantic and affluent population. Ferrari was barely selling any road cars at all, relative to European giants like Fiat. This was all sustainable in the small-scale prewar economy, but after the war it was a road to ruin for Ferrari. Enzo couldn't make the business work on his own, so he started looking for help—which really meant that he wanted to locate a partner who would fund the Scuderia and bask in the glory of that undertaking, while aiding in the manufacture, distribution, and marketing of road cars.

This was where Ford came in. The setup seemed perfect. The Deuce owned a Ferrari, a gift from Enzo himself. He was perhaps unique among Americans in understanding exactly what Ferrari was all about, recognizing that Enzo's Achilles' heel as an auto-maker was that he didn't really want to be an automaker. Race cars were something special. Road cars were a means to an end for Enzo Ferrari, and that end was more race cars.

There was a whiff of arrogance about that, but if anyone in the world was entitled to a little hubris, it was Enzo Ferrari, then in his sixties and not exactly equipped to be the master of Ferrari's next necessary stage, which was to become a global car brand trading on its spectacular successes on the track. His son Alfredo, called Dino, had died in 1956; this was the greatest tragedy and setback of Enzo's life, robbing him of an heir. He had another son, by his mistress, but putting him in charge of the company was an impossibility. (Enzo would finally claim Piero as his son in the late 1970s, and today Piero is the only living Ferrari, holding a 10 percent stake in the company. He became incredibly wealthy when Ferrari separated from Fiat Chrysler Automobiles in 2015 with an initial public offering that valued the carmaker at nearly $10 billion.)

Something about Ford as a great family business appealed to Enzo. Yes, the American colossus had held a public stock offering in the mid-1950s, but the Ford family still ran the show. Enzo Ferrari believed that Henry Ford II would understand what he required, which was to become for all practical purposes the European racing arm of Ford, using victories on the track to sell more and more sexy road cars, especially in the United States. Chinetti was confident that the impeccable Italian style of the Prancing Horse could captivate anyone with the means to spend lavishly. The war had ended—Americans weren't provincial anymore. Many of them had seen Europe during the war and were traveling there. They ruled the world and were getting richer and richer every year. It was a land of new millionaires, and they needed to display their wealth. What better way to do that than with an exciting car that could trace its lineage to epic wins on the track? Ferrari even called one of his cars "California," in a nod to all the Golden State represented: boundless optimism, beautiful weather, Hollywood, gorgeous women, handsome men, pioneers, sunshine, beaches, and roads that went on forever, all leading to sunsets over the Pacific.

In his 2009 book *Go Like Hell: Ford, Ferrari, and Their Battle for Speed and Glory at Le Mans*, A. J. Baime hints that Enzo may have had an ulterior motive in courting Ford. Ferrari had been involved relatively recently in a crash that had cost the lives of both a driver and fourteen spectators at the Formula One grand prix race at Monza, near Milan, in northern Italy's industrial region, and Enzo had abruptly become a national pariah, a menace. He had to do something to change the climate in which he lived, given that he was otherwise widely regarded as a national treasure, and Ferrari the automaker was a potent symbol of Italy's recovery from the war and fascism. (There has never been a less fascist machine than a sinuous red Ferrari, brimming with decadent Western values and a disdain for Aryan *Übermensch* propaganda.)

Is it possible that Enzo was playing Henry for short-term reputational rehabilitation?

I don't think so. Enzo could see that he needed a sugar daddy, and he did get one later, when Fiat took effective control of Ferrari in the 1970s. That was obviously more nationalistically palatable, as Fiat was the symbol of the Italian postwar economic come-back, overseen by a patrician family headed by the peerless Gianni Agnelli—the only man in Italy who had anything on Enzo Ferrari. As the deal making progressed with Ford and rapidly went off the rails, it became abundantly clear that all Enzo wanted, down deep, was to keep the Scuderia going. The rest was noise, vulgar commerce. Enzo wasn't really a natural businessman—he was a *driver*, a merchant of speed, who built the machines that most gloriously accessed that twentieth-century creation.

It's not really clear whether the Deuce overplayed his hand or if Ford simply over-bureaucratized the process of buying Enzo's life work, without properly grasping why it *was* his lifework. But when it came time to sign the papers for a proposed $10 million acquisition of Ferrari by Ford, Enzo quickly spotted that Ford might—*might*—have something to say about racing investment. And that was that.

Here's what Enzo wanted: 100 percent control of the Scuderia. Ford would buy the road-car operation and expand it. And the money would flow back to Enzo, and he would use it to build race cars, co-branded as Ferraris and Fords, that would win the 24 Hours of Le Mans and Formula One races. Or maybe just Le Mans, or whatever, ultimately, Enzo thought was right. He would have no master when it came to racing.

It was an astonishingly naive approach to the deal. But Enzo thought Ford understood. They were a company, and a family, that had built the Model T and sold it to everybody. Ferrari was a company, and a family, that built race cars and didn't care about selling cars to anybody.

The thing is, in defining Ford as just a brute manufacturer of transportation for the masses, Enzo overlooked a small but relevant detail. The first Henry Ford, the founder of the company, had been a race-car driver. Like Enzo, he understood the marketing value of speed—of one car being able to beat another.

"He used his winnings from a race to start Ford," Mark Fields reminded me in Le Mans.

In October 1901, Henry Ford took part in the only race he would ever win. He defeated Alexander Winton in a ten-lap contest (shortened from twenty-five) in Grosse Pointe, near Detroit, with $1,000 on the line. In a race that would predate the 24 Hours of Le Mans by decades, Ford won with reliability. Winton's car exceeded Ford's by forty horsepower, but Ford's own design made it to the finish, while Winton's faltered.

The thirty-eight-year-old Henry Ford was coming off a failed automotive venture and needed investors to start the new Ford Motor Company. His win against Winton convinced them that Ford would make good on his promises. By 1903, the Ford Motor Company had been established.

It all started with a race. Not much of race, to be sure, nothing that would have impressed Enzo all that much. But still, a race. Who knows whether the Deuce was channeling that victory, sixty-some years after the fact, when he got word that Enzo had rebuffed his offer. But something in Henry Ford II rose up at the thought that Ferrari had no respect for Ford's racing potential, something deep-seated and based in its own way on racing pride.

Enzo didn't need Ford? Then Henry Ford II would show Enzo he wasn't as good at racing as he thought. "All right, we'll beat his ass"—that was what Henry II reportedly said when the deal went bust. The Ford GT40 was about to be born. And the place Henry Ford II would choose to beat Enzo Ferrari was the site of Ferrari's greatest success: Le Mans.

Chapter 6 ≡≡≡
No Tougher Test

It's not easy for anyone living in the early twenty-first century to understand what speed meant to someone living in the early twentieth. Just two decades before the running of the first 24 Hours of Le Mans, "speed" meant a particularly fast horse or a ship that could go perhaps 17 knots (about 20 miles per hour). The first automobiles were clattering, modified equestrian coaches with small motors. They were faster than walking, and faster than bicycles. But to the modern eye, they were alarmingly slow.

The fastest machines of the day were trains and, as the new century progressed, airplanes. A train powered by steam wouldn't hit 100 miles per hour until 1934, a mark set by the legendary Flying Scotsman, known for its runs from London to Edinburgh. Airplanes in the early twentieth century were also crossing the once-mythic 100-mph barrier: the Sopwith Camel biplane, which achieved fame in the skies over England and France during World War I, had a top speed of 113 miles per hour.

Of course, all this relative speed for citizens of the pre– and post–WWI era was a revelation. It did more than improve their lives and add danger, romance, and glamour to the most exciting products of the technological revolution—it redefined consciousness by altering humanity's relationship with time. What once took weeks, it was apparent, could now take days, or hours. High-speed transatlantic crossings were in the cards; after World War I, Nazi Germany would build huge zeppelin airships that could beat a luxury liner from Europe to America. Faraway cities and towns were now much more accessible. And it wasn't necessary to feed, groom, and attend to the flesh-and-blood health issues of an automobile. A car required a mechanic, not a veterinarian, and if you blew a tire, you didn't have to consider shooting your car to put it out of its misery. It might have been a less noble form of transportation, but it redefined life.

Almost as soon as cars arrived on the scene, people started to race them, as Henry Ford had in that Michigan race designed to drum up funding for the future Ford Motor Company. By the 1920s, it was abundantly evident that fast cars made for a thrilling spectacle, and a culture of racing grew up around them. But these cars were often purpose-built for the track or the racecourse, or at least seriously modified, as were the road cars Enzo Ferrari built for well-heeled enthusiasts of his true passion, racing.

Le Mans represented a different challenge: to build fast cars that could go the distance. Speed *and* reliability mattered. A race car could impress for the distance and time span of a grand prix race, but how about a car that could handle an *entire day* of uninter-rupted punishment? That, it was reasoned, would be a car worth owning—and the automakers that gave society those cars would be worth buying from.

The first 24 Hours of Le Mans—known in France as the 24 Heures du Mans—was held in 1923, in the very early days of motor racing. It didn't take long for Le Mans to cement its reputation as the premier endurance-racing event in the world (being first cer-tainly helped). A French team of two drivers won the first race, in 1923, but the host country was dethroned the following year by a team from Britain. The Italians and Alfa Romeo would become contenders and champions in the early 1930s. The race would be interrupted by a strike in 1936 and then by World War II; during the war, the venue had been turned into a Luftwaffe base by the Nazis, with the Mulsanne Straight pressed into service as a runway, leading to its bombing by the Allies. Basic repairs delayed the track's return to use until 1949, when Le Mans was both revived and modernized as an important date on the motorsports calendar.

The 1949 race was notable for several reasons. First, it was won by Luigi Chinetti, driving a very early postwar Ferrari racer, the 166. His victory would establish Ferrari at Le Mans for the coming decades, and set up Chinetti, who had left Italy, to become Enzo Ferrari's point man in the United States, which would eventually grow to become the carmaker's largest market. The 1949 comeback race was marred by crashes and a death (Pierre Maréchal, a Brit, who drove his Aston Martin without brakes until he finally and tragically wrecked it), but that was Le Mans, a dangerous contest. The competitors, and for that matter all of liberated France, were patriotically thrilled to witness the return of the race.

The postwar period also meant that Le Mans would be professionalized. Military technologies would come into play; if the people of Europe had thought World War I biplanes were fast at 113 miles per hour, the arrival of P-51 Mustang fighters in the skies over Europe, escorting bombers into Germany, was a revelation: they could crack 400 miles per hour with ease. The Le Mans cars began to more closely resemble what we now commonly think of as a "Le Mans racer"—a sports car with highly aerodynamic bodywork and a closed cockpit for the driver, versus the open design of the prewar years.

From roughly 1950 to 1970, Le Mans was a high-risk venue for drivers and spectators alike. After eighty-plus fans were killed in a 1955 crash, the Automobile Club de l'Ouest (ACO), the organizing entity, began to make major changes, implementing a now-familiar separation of spectators from the dangers of racing.

Racing legends were made during this twenty-year stretch. American driver Phil Hill won at Le Mans for the first time in 1958 and again in 1961. New Zealander Bruce McLaren, who was in the winning Ford GT40 in 1966, would go on to build race cars and give his name to a winning Formula One team and a line of supercars and hypercars in the 1990s (McLaren himself died in a crash in 1970). Belgian racer Jacky Ickx won at Le Mans six times between 1969 and 1982. The Englishman Derek Bell won five times, once in the mid-1970s and then four times in the 1980s. And American legend A. J. Foyt took a Le Mans crown in a Ford GT40 in 1967 with fellow American Dan Gurney; Foyt is the only driver to have captured motor racing's most prestigious quartet: the Indy 500, the Daytona 500, and the twenty-four-hour races at both Le Mans and Daytona.

Le Mans also caught the imagination of Hollywood, although the most famous on-screen depiction of the race, Steve McQueen's *Le Mans*, from 1971, was a box-office disaster. Its production had been beset with delays, screenplay rewrites, director changes, and an actual crash during filming, in which British pro driver David Piper was so severely injured that he had to have the lower part of one leg amputated. McQueen was not just a Tinseltown fan of Le Mans—his original plan for the film had been to drive the actual race, sharing seat time with the Scottish legend Jackie Stewart. McQueen had aimed to follow up on his second-place finish, with Peter Revson, at the 1970 12 Hours of Sebring in Florida, which he drove with his broken foot in a cast. To prevent the Hollywood icon's Porsche from nabbing a first at Sebring, Mario Andretti made a late car switch to a second Ferrari competing in the race, and took the win.

McQueen created the most enduring cinematic testament to the reality of Le Mans. Another actor, Patrick Dempsey, has actually driven in the race and gone to the podium to accept a trophy. He finished second with his own team, Dempsey-Proton Racing, in a Le Mans GT class in 2015. He has run the 24 Hours four times since 2009.

The 1970s and '80s were a great period for auto racing in general, but an explosion in popularity meant that Le Mans was thrown into competition for mind share with a dizzying range of other major motorsports events, from Formula One to the Indy 500 to various sports-car contests. The impact of NASCAR's evolution into a monumental spectacle, and ultimately America's favorite type of racing, shouldn't be underestimated.

It was in this period that Cale Yarborough, a recently retired NASCAR legend, brought a big, rude stock car, a Camaro, to Le Mans. The story was entertainingly recounted by Bob Ottum in *Sports Illustrated* in 1981. "The Camaro looks as if it might have been picked up from some raggedy-pants U.S. trackside and plopped right down in the infield paddock at Le Mans, smack in among the sleek Lolas and glittering Ferraris and some Porsche prototypes so functionally streamlined that they look like horizontal teardrops," Ottum wrote. "Spectators and other drivers are strolling around to look at the Camaro. There is a great deal of Gallic shrugging and rolling of eyes."

(For what it's worth, Ottum's piece, from the heyday of *Sports Illustrated*, turned me on to the possibilities of journalism set free from the "just the facts" constraints of newspaper reporting. I read about Yarborough's ill-fated thirteen-lap stint at Le Mans in the Camaro—which could top 200 miles per hour on the Mulsanne—with a rapt attention bordering on the obsessive. I read it at least a dozen times, digesting every change of pace, every stylistic flourish, and every incongruous pitting of the big, loud American car against the snazzy, sexy European machines.)

The closing decades of the twentieth century were also when the most significant change was made to the Circuit de la Sarthe itself. It became clear in the late 1980s that prototype cars of increasingly immense horsepower were treating the Mulsanne Straight in the same way that a Saturn V rocket treated liftoff.

Didier Theys told me about his first Le Mans, which was in 1982. "On one of the long straightaways of five miles, I was in a Porsche prototype and I was going 245 miles per hour," he said. It was the fastest the man had ever moved in his entire life, at least on the ground. But he wasn't afraid—not exactly. At that speed, a different state of consciousness appears. You could call it resignation, but not of the depressive variety. Rather, it is a resignation born of extreme rationality, manifesting itself against the obvious urge toward terror. "Every time you're over 180 mph," Theys said, "You're just a passenger behind the steering wheel."

And Le Mans was always, initially, jarring. "There was really no other racetrack like Le Mans in the 1980s," Theys noted. "You'd get in the car for the first time, hit the long straight, hold onto the wheel, and say 'Shit! This is fast!'" But practice soothed the nerves. "On the next lap, it's more like slow motion. Then by the third lap you start to see more. And by the fourth lap, your body has adapted."

Think about that for a moment. Race-car drivers train their entire lives to both control and accept their machines. The best racing happens when the driver can unleash the unstable beast that his car can be, much as a jockey will release a thoroughbred horse when the final turn is in sight. But although a driver might go flat out, he or she (racing in the twenty-first century isn't entirely the boys' club it was for its first 100 years) always keeps a sliver of control in the pocket of the fireproof racing suit, a way to pull back from the brink. It wasn't like that in the old days at Le Mans. If you weren't willing to take on 245 miles per hour, you could be sure that the guy behind you was, which meant you would probably lose.

Joey Hand, who had briefly led at the 2016 Daytona in his Ford GT before mechanical failures started to mount, said something similar. For him, Le Mans was an *initiation*.

"Le Mans is one of those places you can't respect until you do it," he said. "You know, I could tell myself that I've done Daytona, so I can do Le Mans." But Le Mans is an order of magnitude different from Daytona.

"Le Mans is high intensity, all the time," Hand said, his American English cheerfully unaccented. He could be from anywhere, could probably have done anything. But he chose to become a professional driver. ("Since I was eleven years old, I've driven racing vehicles as fast as I can," he said. "That's what I do.") In 2011, Hand won Daytona with Chip Ganassi in a prototype car, then took third at Le Mans with BMW in the GTE Pro class. Now he was heading for another turn on the dance floor.

"Le Mans is a white-knuckle situation," he said. The GT cars aren't set up with a lot of downforce, so their tires can't grip as much in the corners. "You're more hanging in than anything else," he said. "And that's just driving your own car. You also need to deal with getting passed by the prototypes"—more than fifty cars of different classes are all racing at the same time. "Your eyes are popping out of your head."

But after 1990, when the Mulsanne was broken up by the "chicanes" that were intended to constrain speeds on what was becoming, even by the grim standards of Le Mans, just too deadly, the golden period that had lasted since roughly the mid-1960s seemed to have been wrung out, and Le Mans drifted. As competition thinned out in the prototype class, and big car companies limited their commitments to sports-car racing, the stage was set for Audi to exert an awesome influence over Le Mans, first with its R8 prototype (the name found its way to a V-10 mid-engine supercar) and later with an innovative turbo-diesel prototype that would spend half a decade dueling with Peugeot's own diesel-powered cars.

Diesel engines hadn't yet made an impact at Le Mans, but in the early twenty-first century they suddenly became the only way to win in the prototype class (the sports-car classes stuck with good old-fashioned high-octane racing gasoline). In the 2010s, yet another technological innovation appeared at Le Mans: diesel-electric hybrids. Audi added the technology to its serially victorious TDI diesel designs, but in 2015 Porsche jumped into the party. Using its own innovative gas-electric hybrid, the 919 took down its corporate sibling (Porsche and Audi are both part of the VW Group) in a new class, LMP1-H, created to address the arrival of the exotic new hybrid engines.

The early twenty-first century has been a good one for Le Mans for one key reason: the 2000s and 2010s have shown that the Circuit de la Sarthe has lost none of its capacity to validate intricate, sophisticated new propulsion systems in a trial-by-endless-fire scenario. The most advanced racing engines now are not found in NASCAR, Formula One, or IndyCar machines—they're found, as it seems they always should be, in Le Mans cars.

Modern-day endurance racing and the twenty-first-century version of Le Mans present some challenges that the old-timers never directly faced. One of these is, in fact, the existence of two general classes of cars on the track (prototype and GT), one of which brings vastly more power and technology to the table. Different types of cars have always taken part in the race, but only in the last two decades have the prototypes become so powerful

Henry Ford (left) only ran one race in his life, but he won it, defeating Alexander Winton. It was 1901, and there wasn't yet a Ford Motor Company.

Ford won the race because his less powerful car was more reliable than Winton's, which failed before the ten-lap race ended.

Henry Ford II could have lived a life of leisure. Instead, he took control of the Ford Motor Company and by the early 1960s, he set his sights on beating Ferrari.

Ford's early GT40s tasted defeat at Le Mans. Here's a GT40 Mark I passing under the famous Dunlop Bridge in 1964.

By the 1965 Le Mans campaign, former winner Carroll Shelby had taken over Ford's effort.

A huge new 7.0-liter V-8 engine would propel the GT40 Mark IIs to victory at Le Mans in 1966. Handling was sacrificed for raw speed.

The GT40 got its name because it was so low: just forty inches tall.

The GT40 wins at Daytona in 1966, beginning the assault on
Le Mans that would come later in the year.

Dan Gurney was one of the Ford drivers who would pilot the GT40
around the demanding Circuit de la Sarthe in 1966.

The dangerous "Le Mans" start.
The drivers had to run to their cars,
start them, and quickly get up to
speed. Buckling in was a waste of
precious time.

Chris Amon and Bruce McLaren were
the 1966 Ford drivers who immortalized
McLaren's phrase "Go like hell!"

The legendary finish at the 1966 24 Hours of Le Mans.

The 1966 finish was controversial. Ford wanted a tie for the two GT40s driven by Ken Miles and Denny Hulme and Bruce McLaren and Chris Amon. But McLaren and Amon had started farther back, so race officials decided that they had covered the greater distance and should get a win. Miles was incensed.

Enzo Ferrari built his legend from auto racing. He sold road cars so that he could build race cars—and Le Mans was his playground in the 1960s.

Carroll Shelby alongside a pair of his race cars. Shelby and his band of hot-rodders guided Ford to victory in 1966.

Another Le Mans win for Ford followed in 1967, and the company headquarters in Dearborn was illuminated accordingly.

Prior to the new GT in 2015, Ford created a supercar in 2005 that bore the famous name.

The Ford GT's designer, Moray Callum.

The 2005 GT, being sculpted as a clay model by Ford's designers.

Alan Mulally wasn't a "car guy" when he became Ford's CEO in 2006, but the former Boeing executive saved the automaker from bailout and bankruptcy.

Alan Mulally joins Stephen Colbert on *The Colbert Report* to talk about the Mustang in 2013.

Current Ford CEO Mark Fields alongside the new GT supercar.

When the new GT was unveiled at the 2015 North American International
Auto Show in Detroit, jaws dropped throughout the car world.
From left to right: Bill Ford, executive chairman, Ford Motor Company;
Mark Fields, president and chief executive officer; Joe Hinrichs,
executive vice president and president, The Americas; Raj Nair, group
vice president and chief technical officer, Global Product Development.

Dave Pericak was put in charge of
Ford Performance and the GT
Le Mans campaign after reinventing
the all-important Mustang. He
would endure the highest highs
and the lowest lows.

Racing team owner Chip Ganassi
brought decades of experience to
Ford's return to big-time endurance
racing. Could he live up to
Carroll Shelby's legacy?

The GT was first shown in blue, but later began to make the rounds of the auto show circuit in other colors, including a breathtaking white in 2016.

Bill Ford and his new baby. He inherited his family's racing legacy, established at Le Mans in the 1960s by Henry Ford II. But Bill Ford also had to steer Ford through the financial crisis, as CEO and later as chairman.

Ford created a small, snap-together model of the GT. I have one in my home.

The racing version of the GT was built by Multimatic in Canada and had to be rapidly tested on the track before it could make its racing debut in early 2016.

The buzz around the new GT race car prompted LEGO to create a special version.

Ford's racing simulator was the centerpiece of the carmaker's Performance Technical Center in North Carolina. Drivers were able to take virtual practice laps around the Le Mans course.

Rain hampered the start of the 2016 24 Hours of Le Mans, but the bad weather disappeared after about an hour and conditions remained good for the rest of the race.

Giancarlo Fisichella proved that when it came to race-car driving for Ferrari, he was willing to bleed red.

Ferraris ran in several racing classes at the 2016 24 Hours of Le Mans.
The Scuderia Corsa number 62 car won the GTE-Am class.

Both AF Corse Ferraris failed to finish in the GTE-Pro class, but the number 82
Risi Competizione 488 GTE captured second after a spectacular duel with Ford.

The team that can make the fewest pit stops—to refuel, change tires,
or make repairs—will often win Le Mans.

Fifty years to the day after Ford's 1-2-3 1966 win, Ford's GT racers went 1-3-4.
Once again, it had been Ford versus Ferrari. But in 2016, Ferrari fought to the end.

Four GTs in total took the Circuit de la Sarthe in France for the 24 Hours of Le Mans: two from North America, and two from Europe.

Ford crosses the finish line first at the 2016 24 Hours of Le Mans.

It was one of the greatest days in Ford's history when the 2016 24 Hours of Le Mans trophy came back to Dearborn for a celebration with Ford's employees.

Back in Dearborn, Ford celebrated with style.

The GT's drivers won races before and after Le Mans.

and technologically advanced that they have to establish an uneasy détente with the rest of the field.

The prototypes and the GT cars aren't really racing against each other, although the vehicle that turns the most laps over the allotted time frame—always a prototype, given the superior speed of that class—officially wins the race. Under these conditions, the difficulty of managing a car at frighteningly high speeds isn't the first thing on a driver's mind, especially if he or she is running in the GT class.

"The first challenge is traffic," Theys explained to me. Theys always raced prototype cars at Le Mans, and for him, racing alongside the GTs presented some tactical difficulties. "You're running at different speeds, especially in corners. So you can catch a GT, but then you have to ask yourself if you should dive into the apex of the corner to catch him or pass." The apex is the "center" of the turn; it represents a center point a driver aims for to create the straightest racing line possible through a curve, to sustain speed and shorten the length of a lap, thereby improving time.

This might not sound like a big deal, but when a race can be won by a small fraction of a full lap, it's actually critical to deal correctly and opportunistically with the traffic issues. "If you wait two corners, the guy who's two seconds behind you will be in your tailpipe," Theys told me.

"Between GT and prototype, there needs to be a respect. It's not that the drivers aren't as good," Theys said, dismissing a common endurance-racing stigma, the assumption that the best drivers get the prototype seats, while the ones who've lost their edge and are just hanging on, or those starting out, man the GT cars. "Each guy has his own race," Theys stressed.

A sort of mutual respect does indeed tend to develop, based on the degree to which racing drivers are the best judges of the mechanical aspects of their machines. Nobody understands physics quite like the professionals who live it, at the levels of speed most people experience only when taking off in a jetliner.

"A prototype car can go around a GT very easily," Theys said. But the inverse isn't even remotely the case. A GT car has less downforce and is heavier. "So once a driver commits to a line going into a corner, he can't change."

For a prototype driver, that makes passing in traffic a simple, binary decision. "Either I go for it," Theys said, "or I'm patient."

Beyond the thousand small yet critical decisions during a race that lasts all day and all night, another factor comes into play at Le Mans. "You really need to trust the car at that speed," Theys said. "And you have to trust the team that built the car, the team in the pits, and the people who supply the critical parts. I've had friends who lost their lives at Le Mans because a tire failed, or had something go wrong and they found themselves upside down in a tree."

The crashes at Le Mans can truly come out of almost nowhere, grimly punctuating the imperative of turning steady, error-free laps. Theys recalled a devastating crash in 1999. "That was my first year with the Audi factory team, and we were under a yellow [caution] flag, but I couldn't see anything for two laps, and I got on the radio and found out that the crash had happened in the Indianapolis corner."

The Indianapolis corner occurs after the Mulsanne Straight. "I couldn't see the flipped car," Theys said. He couldn't see it because the Scottish driver Peter Dumbreck had gone airborne in his Mercedes at 190 miles per hour, and then flipped over three times into the trees adjacent to the roadway. Miraculously, he walked away from the crash.

"That's Le Mans," Theys said. "It's high speed."

Danger mixed with exhaustion mixed with significant technological innovation—that combination is what makes Le Mans Le

Mans and has kept the race relevant since the early 1920s. There is also the inalienable Frenchness of the event, the way it articulates a specifically Gallic claim to an *idea* about auto racing—that it should be very fast and impressively grueling, not dissimilar to the Tour de France. For the French, life is a combination of inimitable flair and dutiful struggle. You want to look good while you're complaining about your miserable lot.

Even the Le Mans weather can be an ordeal. Because the race is held in June, it can get extremely hot in the cars for the drivers. But it also typically rains. So you struggle to drive your high-performance race car through the night, in the wet, with your windshield wipers on. The spectators get drenched, but they cheer the circus anyway, as they collectively concoct a sort of automotive version of a big music festival out of a damp day in the French countryside listening to the savage roar of fast machines pushing their limits. For the French, this is a party, as it has been since the 1920s.

On the track and in the pits, it definitely isn't a party. It's serious business. The race is, at that level, all about keeping the car running for twenty-three hours so that it can be there at the end to win in the twenty-fourth. Drivers have to pick their spots and avoid risky passes but not skip out on obvious opportunities. They are usually in constant strategic conversation on the radio with their teams in the pits. Nightfall adds a conservative, position-holding element to the driving, but it also demands that the teams switch the risk-taking back on at dawn.

But they can't take too much risk. A mistake, even a minor one, can mean a trip to the garage and the loss of several laps, which over the course of twenty-four hours, remarkably, can be enough to bring decisive defeat. The circuit is also sprawling and long, so it can be difficult for teams to have a strong sense of where their cars are on the course.

A win at Le Mans meant that a manufacturer and a racing team had survived a profound test. That was why, in the 1960s, Ferrari was so proud of its dominance on the Circuit de la Sarthe. It was also why Ford chose Le Mans, never having run the race before, to make its mark on European racing.

Chapter 7

The GT40

If given the opportunity, I could probably jump into the new Ford GT race car and get around the Circuit de la Sarthe in passable fashion. It's not *that* different from the road car, or from any other modern supercar that's been modified for racing. The tricky part would be getting used to driving in a racing suit, wearing a helmet and gloves. The car has a dual-clutch transmission that makes shifting gears fairly simple; there's no clutch on the floor. It has power steering. There's even a hydration system, for sending fluids along a tube to the helmet. The biggest challenge would be getting comfortable in the snug interior, but I'm not a big guy, and tight little sports cars have never been a problem for me.

The GT40 that raced at Le Mans is a completely different story. To a twenty-first-century sensibility—to people raised on technology, never far from central air-conditioning—the rudimentary nature of a 1960s race car is borderline appalling. Cars were basically all engine and tires, with the body shaped as tightly around those two elements as possible. Driver comfort and ergonomics matter nowadays, but in the mid-1960s, if you complained that a car wasn't comfortable, you could quit being a real driver and explore job prospects for chauffeurs. The GT40 was true to this harsh ideal. The enormous engine filled the entire rear of the car. The tires were huge. The rest of the car, including the driver, was just along for the ride.

And what a ride it was. At 2,682 pounds, the GT40 was only slightly heavier than a Mini Cooper, the small car recently created by BMW as an homage to the influential original Mini designed by Alec Issigonis in the late 1950s. But Mini Coopers don't put out 485 horsepower, or attempt to surpass 200 miles per hour on the Mulsanne Straight. There were several reasons the GT40 won Le Mans four years in a row in the mid- to late 1960s, and speed was definitely one of them. The car was just so, so fast.

There's a place called Classic Car Club in Manhattan—a sort of hyper-elevated rental-car agency for automotive enthusiasts who are willing to pay big bucks to have new McLarens and vintage Porsches at their disposal. Operating out of a warehouse on the Hudson River, with an Airstream trailer for an office, Classic Car Club also has a replica GT40. It's not the real thing, but a close approximation, done up in the famous Gulf livery that motorsports enthusiasts are obsessed with, a combination of turquoise and orange.

The first thing you notice about the GT40 is that it's *small*. You expect such a historic machine, even a copy, to be imposing—but it isn't. That's because it's about the size of a modern compact sedan and is essentially a thin shell of aerodynamic sheet metal wrapped around a lightweight skeleton, with a massive V-8 engine dropped in behind the driver's head. Enormous tires complete the picture.

It's a beautiful thing, but in a way blunt. You can gaze upon a sculptural Jaguar E-Type—which Enzo Ferrari called the most beautiful car ever—or a fiberglass-bodied Corvette from the *Boogie Nights* era of the 1970s, or a Porsche 911 from the 1980s, or a Lamborghini Miura, or a Dino Ferrari (named for Enzo's deceased son), or even many of the lovely Ferrari road cars designed by Pininfarina and built in the 1950s and '60s that now fetch tens of millions at auctions, and you may respond as if you're appreciating an authentic piece of fine art.

I've never been able to do that with the GT40. Its beauty is more rude, purposeful. The new GT, by contrast, is a stunner, with a far more attractive design than its illustrious forebear had. The flying buttresses and the tightly sweeping lines of the rear end guarantee that. It's a car with drama.

The GT40 has often been described as "industrial." It contrasted vividly with the Ferrari 330 P3, at least visually. Under the hood, the rival cars for the 1966 running of Le Mans were very different, with Ford's immense 7.0-liter V-8 outclassing the 330's 4.0-liter V-12. But on the outside, the 330 P3 was everything that makes a Ferrari a Ferrari. (The *P* stands for "prototype," which in the 1960s was the vehicle class that, as today, aimed for outright wins in Le Mans and other endurance races; the GT40 would also compete in this class, even though it carried the "GT" name.) The 330 was, naturally, *rosso corsa*, but it was also an elegant combination of the fine-boned and the utterly burly, with a delicate and curvaceous front end flowing boldly up to form the powerful front fenders before tucking in over the doors, then surging upward again to form the even more powerful rear haunches. The windshield was almost a half bubble, and the roof curved smoothly down over the engine compartment in a fastback style, ending at the integrated rear spoiler. It was a magnificent essay in Italian racing design, visual poetry carved from aluminum.

Next to *that* the GT40 looked like a slab of metal, albeit with a pair of arrogant hood scoops. The 330 P3 delivered the impression that it would obliterate all comers on the track, simply by conquering them with beauty. Its sheer prettiness was daunting. And its predecessors had set a standard, winning Le Mans from 1960 to 1965. That run included triumphs in the face of Ford's first efforts with its new GT cars, the early Mark I versions, which tackled Le Mans unsuccessfully in 1964 and 1965. (Those cars ran with smaller engines, displacing 4.2 liters.)

What really distinguished the GTs from the Ferrari aesthetically was that the Ferraris were holistic in their design and engineering attitude, with the bodywork and the engine and the wheels and tires all adding up to a create an impression far greater than the sum of their parts. The GTs, meanwhile, were designed and built in England, with Ford engines provided; they could be more accurately described as "platforms" for racing, relying on a tried-and-true formula. A small, lightweight, aerodynamic chassis was combined with a big engine to produce speed, and lots of it. Sure, there were also reliability and handling to consider, but the basics were the basics. Besides, Ford didn't have time to overthink the design, and as it turned out, the platform supplied an unexpected level of flexibility.

The initial GT40s, the Mark I models, were a disappointment, performing poorly in 1964, with Le Mans a total wash. This was when Carroll Shelby joined up, displacing his former racing partner, John Wyer, the Englishman who had overseen the first GT40 Le Mans campaign.

Shelby was an experienced driver—he had won Le Mans in 1959, in an Aston Martin—and an automotive innovator. His first creation was the AC Cobra, an utterly bonkers car that was both devastatingly attractive and comically fast. As the Mark I racers were faltering in 1964, Shelby's Cobra won the GT class. That car was something of a general template for the first GT40s, in that it was a lightweight AC roadster with a 4.7-liter Ford V-8 under the hood up front. And it got Shelby—a Texas chicken farmer, who had a taste for speed, the talent to construct great cars and win races in Europe, and an iron will forged from overcoming a sickly childhood—noticed in Dearborn.

In addition to the Cobra and the GT40, Shelby would develop a series of high-performance Mustangs for Ford. These cars have lived on in Ford's contemporary portfolio since the early 2000s, with big engines and Cobra badging. Along the way, Shelby, who passed away in 2012 at the age of eighty-nine, also participated in the development of one of the wildest sports cars ever conceived in Detroit, the Dodge Viper. The long-hooded, low-to-the-ground beast debuted in 1992, with a massive 8.0-liter V-10 cranking out 400 horsepower, which at the time was dismaying power.

Shelby notoriously had a bum heart, even as far back as the early 1960s. But that didn't stop him from taking up the charge for Ford to beat Ferrari at Le Mans. Shelby knew what the secret was to a winning Le Mans car, but his knowledge wouldn't yield victory until 1966, two years after the first GT40 Mark I hit the Circuit de la Sarthe. For several years, Shelby would struggle with unreliable early versions of the GT40.

One of the secrets he had hit upon was in the brakes. More accurately, it was how quickly the brakes could be changed. Again, as with so much about Le Mans, it came down to the Mulsanne Straight. It was just over three and a half miles, run at speeds clocking at 200-plus miles per hour. At the end of it, a tight corner forced drivers to saw their speed in half. Again and again, the brakes were subjected to perhaps the single most demanding challenge for brakes ever devised.

The stresses were so severe in the 1960s that the rotors—the cast-iron plates that the calipers clamp onto to slow the car—could crack. And a race car without brakes isn't much of a race car. Braking really is the secret sauce of competitive driving; the pros don't hold back on speed when they have the chance to run flat out, but on winding, twisting road courses (as opposed to high-speed ovals), they need superb and reliable brakes, because they quite literally slam them down without hesitation. From Shelby's perspective, the brakes made all the difference.

With the driver and a full fuel load of just over forty gallons, the GT40s weighed about 4,000 pounds, and most of the weight was engine. As Shelby explained, the kinetic energy built up on the Mulsanne, and the braking demand on the hard corner at the end of it, would destroy the brakes in two or three hours.

"You really had to manage the brakes, because at the end of the Mulsanne Straight they would be cold and then subjected to tremendous heat as you slowed from 220 mph," said Chris Amon, who had shared the driving with Bruce McLaren in the winning GT40 in 1966.

So Ford had a choice: design a longer-lasting braking system or figure out how to change the brakes faster. The latter won out. Shelby credited Phil Remington, whom he called an "old hot rodder," with coming up with a way to switch out the brakes in a minute. Endurance races in the 1960s pivoted on little things like that.

Shelby's tale of what actually captured the Le Mans wins back then is also indicative of how the mid-1960s assault was a frustrating, fitful undertaking. The 1964 and 1965 cars weren't equal to the monumental task at hand. Life was indeed slower in those days, even as America raced the Soviets to put a man on the moon. Memos were still typed. People sent letters in the mail. Computers were the size of rooms. Air travel was a novelty, although a new global "jet set" had arrived. A working day was peppered with coffee breaks and smoke breaks, and executives often retired for the afternoon after their three-martini lunches. Henry Ford II didn't hold back on the cigarettes or the scotch. His goal wasn't to beat Ferrari *immediately*. It was to beat Ferrari *soon*, and then to keep on beating him, and to prove that Ford's technologies were just as good as the best the Europeans had to offer.

Ford was prepared to be patient, although the dismal outings of the GT40 Mark I in 1964 and 1965 did bring about the most apparent major change to the car, which was the increase in engine size. Enzo Ferrari didn't worry about this enough, although his lieutenants knew that it would be hard for any European manu-facturer, not just Ferrari, to keep pace with the monster American power plants.

For Shelby and the rest of the engineers continuing to labor away at Henry II's Le Mans objective, the bigger engine was a given.

The GT40 Mark II was, eventually, the game changer. Speed hadn't been the issue for the Mark I—it was on paper and in test-ing faster than the 330 P3. Reliability was. All three GT40 Mark I cars failed to finish Le Mans in 1964.

In 1965, the first two Mark II GT40s with the 7.0-liter V-8 jour-neyed to the Circuit de la Sarthe, joined by several examples of the Mark I entered by non-Ford-factory teams. None finished—the race was won by a North American Ferrari team founded by Enzo's old friend Luigi Chinetti—but Shelby now knew how he could fix the GT40's key mechanical problem. The new V-8 was, understandably, a fuel hog, making for too many pit stops. So it had to get lighter. The GT40's aerodynamics also had to be improved, to keep it on the track, and the gearbox would need to be upgraded to handle the malevolent torque that the big engine was capable of sending to the rear wheels. The GT40 had been steadily tweaked for three years, demonstrating that the basic ar-chitecture of the car was solid and that Ford hadn't been bingeing on hubris in believing that it was possible to go from nowhere to the winner's circle in endurance racing.

The changes could all be swiftly achieved, in time for the begin-ning of the 1966 season, at the first-ever twenty-four-hour race at Daytona. The Florida race would be the ideal test for the Mark II headed into Le Mans, and the revamped car lived up to Shelby's and Ford's ambitions. Ken Miles and Lloyd Ruby drove the car to victory, and anticipation built for a Ford-Ferrari rematch in France six months later.

The bottom line was that Shelby, with Ford's backing, had refused to give up on the car. Maybe there was some personal animosity between the crusty Texan and Enzo Ferrari, a residue from Shelby's racing days. (According to A. J. Baime's book *Go Like Hell*, Shelby considered Enzo a reckless, win-at-all-costs taskmaster, unconcerned about the lives of his drivers.) But ultimately, the creation of the most famous Le Mans racer of all time was deeply American. Problems arose, and problems were solved. The car got better. It was *prepared* to win.

Chapter 8

One-Two-Three

The 24 Hours of Le Mans in 1966 has moved on in the consciousness of even casual racing fans from the status of lore to legend. It has inspired books and spurred Hollywood to make movies about motorsports.

At Ford's Dearborn, Michigan, headquarters, 1966 stands as arguably the automaker's greatest moment, a time when the racetrack and the boardroom operated on the same plane, with the same priorities. The 1966 Le Mans win has come to stand for American self-confidence, for the magical blending of the automobile as a national icon and as an instrument of speed, for the astounding bravery of the men who drove the GT40 Mark IIs in France on that June weekend, for Ford's technological excellence, for Carroll Shelby's determination, and even for Henry Ford's vision in starting the company in the first place, thereby setting the entire glorious thing in motion.

The thing is, when you study the actual race more closely, you realize that Ford had it won almost from the beginning, when the French tricolor flag was waved and the drivers dashed from the pits to the waiting cars on the starting grid—the classic Le Mans start, which was jettisoned in 1970.

(In a tragic piece of Le Mans history, Belgian driver Jacky Ickx made a leisurely stroll to his Ford GT40 in 1969 and took the extra time to completely strap in while the rest of the field tore off. He started in last place and eventually won, but his gesture was a protest against the dangerous Le Mans start. His actions turned out to be prescient, when John Woolfe suffered a fatal crash in his Porsche in the very first lap.)

The main technical issue for the GT40 Mark II cars that would be entered in the race rested with their huge 7.0-liter V-8s. Ford was betting that speed would triumph over handling. The Ferrari 330 P3s were lighter and quicker in the corners, but their engines were *half* as big in terms of displacement. The Ferraris were going to get clobbered on the Mulsanne Straight. But the Fords were also going to have to slow all that extra weight down, and that could send them to the pits for extra brake changes, in addition to the additional stops to refuel.

But there's a saying in automotive circles: "No replacement for displacement." And on the Circuit de la Sarthe, the importance of velocity on the Mulsanne couldn't be overestimated.

The new GT40s had been scaring the living bejesus out of their drivers for months before Le Mans. They were just so very fast. It was a real test of skill to manage all that surging power, those mountains of torque. During Le Mans practice several months earlier, a driver had been cranking out faster and faster laps—with times that would have been impressive in 2016 for the GT Pro class—until he lost control of the car and smashed it to pieces.

But the drivers all knew what they'd signed up for. Because Le Mans was defined by such high speeds, it was known for horrific crashes that maimed or killed drivers. Every single time you got into a Le Mans car, as you strapped in and made that first run through the gears, roaring under the Dunlop Bridge and into the turns known as the Esses that precede the Mulsanne, you took a good hard look at death. And death looked right back and laughed at you, taunted you, said you'd been a stupid, stupid man to pick this job and that the two of you might have a meeting scheduled, quite possibly out there in the French darkness at 200 miles per hour.

Ford and Ferrari both came to Le Mans in force. Eight new GT40 Mark IIs and sixteen drivers formed Ford's army, while the Ferrari fleet consisted of seven 330 P3s and fourteen drivers. For the sake of comparison, the copiously funded Ford factory effort in 2016 would see four GTs and twelve drivers line up on the grid.

Objectively, you had to scrutinize those numbers and conclude that it was a Ford-Ferrari race and that everybody else would be a spectator.

And that's the way it shook out. Henry Ford II served as the starter for the thirty-fourth running of the race, and in the first half, it was a battle between the Ferraris and the Fords, with the Ferraris leading. But by the time Henry II had helicoptered back to his hotel from the track to wait out the night, the rain had started to fall and the Ferraris had started to fail.

Fortunes had been reversed. Now it was Ferrari's new car that was unreliable, while Ford's machines could go the distance. Through the darkness, the Fords bolstered their lead, while the Ferraris collapsed.

By morning, it wasn't even a race anymore. The Ferraris that were left in the contest had no chance of catching the Fords. So the 24 Hours of Le Mans boiled down to a series of frantic political conversations. It was in fact the second political conundrum to emerge during the race. Early on, the GT40 driven by Bruce McLaren and Chris Amon had been shredding Firestone tires. Ford and Firestone were tight, but McLaren—a racing innovator who had just taken the plunge with his own Formula One team—had a deal with Goodyear and was told that if he could convince the

Goodyear reps in attendance to allow him to run on Goodyears, that was his call. McLaren didn't hesitate, and after some quick discussions, he had four Goodyears on his and Amon's GT40.

But daybreak brought the truly challenging politics to the fore— regrettably, they would undermine what could have been one of the most memorable finishes in the history of auto racing.

The Deuce had returned to the circuit, only to encounter a furious debate about how Ford should stage the finish. With winning almost in the bag, the idea was to have the three leading Fords cross the finish line at the same time, on the last lap of the twenty-four hours. This brought up an obvious question: Who should win the race?

In the pits and the paddock, the idea was that no one should. The result would be a tie between the top two cars. The GT40 driven by Ken Miles and Denny Hulme was in front of the Ford helmed by Bruce McLaren and Chris Amon, and another GT40 was a dozen laps farther back. This third car had been entered by Holman & Moody, which was sort of the Multimatic of its day, a specialist racing fabricator that constructed race cars for Ford.

Initially, the fix was in. Ford and the Shelby team were on board, even though they thought that Ken Miles should get a shot at winning the race outright, given that he had taken firsts at Daytona and at a rainy, deadly, chaotic Sebring race earlier in the season. The Holman & Moody GT40 was strategically permitted to catch up to the lead Shelby GT40s in the waning hours of Le Mans; the third car would finish a distant third, but the Fords would cross the line as a group. And then the technicality of all technicalities doomed Ford's publicity stunt.

Race officials informed the racing teams that McLaren and Amon's car had started farther back on the grid than Miles and Hulme's. If the two cars crossed the line at the same instant, the McLaren-Amon GT40 would have traveled a greater distance in the twenty-four-hour period and would therefore be the winner. You win Le Mans by getting in the most laps during the time frame of the race.

That was what Ken Miles thought. But Ford had other ideas, and in any case, even when everyone figured out that the one-two-three photo for the finish wasn't going to reflect an actual three-way tie, it was too late. Miles, a Brit who had come on board as a test driver for Shelby, had become a racing legend in southern California but hadn't made a big name for himself on the world's grandest stages. The year 1966 was his best shot, and he was dismayed that Ford would deny him the triple victory, of Daytona, Sebring, and Le Mans, for something as irrelevant to a driver as a photo op. He had driven hard for a day and a night and into another day.

Miles had bucked authority in his time with the Ford effort; he was a California guy and tight with Shelby. McLaren and Amon, meanwhile, were great drivers, and McLaren was increasingly an international racing celebrity. But they were from New Zealand, a faraway place no one in America had ever heard of. (It was close to Australia, right?)

In the end—and it was a bitter end that has always tainted the result—the drivers followed orders, and Miles came in second while McLaren finished first. It would be Miles's last chance to win the 24 Hours of Le Mans. Just a few months later, he was killed testing a new GT40 prototype in California for Shelby—a faster and more durable model called the J-car. He was forty-seven years old. McLaren would also soon meet his end. He perished in a crash in 1970, also while testing a new car design. He was thirty-two.

Auto racing was appallingly dangerous in the 1960s. Numerous men had died in the years leading up to Ford's win in '66, but in those days, that was considered the price of doing business. It was one of the factors that animated Carroll Shelby's dislike of Enzo Ferrari, but it wasn't as if Shelby didn't play along. The assumption was that if you were a driver, you didn't just know the risks; you welcomed them. Winners didn't just beat the competition—they beat death.

This nihilistic attitude would be forced out of racing by the Scottish driver Jackie Stewart in the 1970s. Stewart demanded that new barriers between the track and the fans be constructed, and that drivers be required to wear seat belts and more advanced helmets. By the 1980s, auto racing had become far safer.

The sad truth is that fans continually over-romanticize the racing era of the 1960s and '70s. Motorsport was on an even footing with other major sports at that time, featuring competitors who captured the public's imagination. Their exploits behind the wheel brought Hollywood stars into the game, men like Steve McQueen and Paul Newman, who actually finished second overall at Le Mans in 1979, driving a Porsche sponsored by Hawaiian Tropic outfitted in wildly colorful livery. Speed had menace, danger, and sexiness—it was like a drug, for a culture that was suffused with drugs.

It took the heroes of this period, the drivers themselves, to force the changes that would give pro racers a much better chance to enjoy a full career and a long family life. The most terrifying tracks were tamed or retired. The racing teams and the manufacturers began to concentrate on driver safety as a *first* priority, building the car out from a safety cage that was designed to remain intact in a crash, while the entire vehicle shredded around the driver, absorbing the deadly energy of a impact. Racing went from being a glamorous cult of death to what it should have been all along— a sublime celebration of speed. To be sure, drivers still die at the wheel. But many more things have to go wrong than in the good old days, when a mere tire puncture could send a man to racing Valhalla.

In 1966, every driver who got behind the wheel expected, in some part of himself, to die. That was the most basic initial emotional obstacle that Miles and McLaren and all the other GT40 racers had to overcome. Soldiers in combat have to deal with something close to that. In 2016, every driver who got behind the wheel expected that his brilliantly designed and engineered car would save his life if the worst that could happen did take place.

Both states of mind freed the drivers to race. But in 1966, if you won Le Mans, your celebration on the podium meant that you toasted your survival. You drank not just to victory but to life. In 2016, if Ford's drivers were the first GTE Pro competitors to take the checkered flag, they would toast a simpler victory. The stakes might not seem as high, but they'd still have driven very, very fast.

PART III

WE'RE GOING TO WIN FROM THE LEAD

Chapter 9

The Tesla Factor

On a balmy March evening in Los Angeles, just three months before the most advanced Ford race car ever built would take to the Circuit de la Sarthe in France, Tesla Motors CEO Elon Musk took to a stage at his electric-car start-up's design center, just a few miles south of Hollywood and the American cinematic dream factory.

Musk was there to pull the cover off a dream that had nothing to do with movie magic. Instead, he sauntered onstage dressed entirely in black and, after some awkward jokes, made a few comments about the impending catastrophe of global warming—one of the multi-billionaire's overriding personal preoccupations and the reason he bought into Tesla in 2004 after making $180 million when eBay acquired PayPal, the electronic payments service he had cofounded. He then proceeded to preside over the rollout of Tesla's much-anticipated Model 3, a mass-market electric vehicle that would sell for $35,000 when it hit Tesla's showrooms in 2017.

Tesla was already selling a pair of game-changing cars: the Model S sedan, which in its most advanced configuration, equipped with the "Ludicrous" acceleration mode, could scorch a zero-to-sixty run in less than three seconds, outrunning supercars from Ferrari and Lamborghini; and the Model X SUV, with its exotic, up-swinging "falcon wing" doors and "bioweapon defense mode" air-filtration system. But these long-range electric vehicles (EVs) sold for $100,000 and up, to a well-heeled elite, including Silicon Valley venture capitalists and titans of finance.

That certainly created useful cash flow for Tesla (if not profits), but it didn't suit Musk's grand vision, which was to accelerate humanity's transition from the era of fossil fuels—an era that had filled the atmosphere with carbon, disrupting weather patterns and making the planet hotter. In early December 2015, Musk gave a speech at the Sorbonne in Paris, in connection with the United Nations Climate Summit, in which he called governments' reluctance to tax the generation of atmospheric carbon the "dumbest science experiment in history" and "madness." He went on to call for a global carbon tax, as he had done several times before.

No chief executive of a traditional automaker would even consider giving a speech like the one Musk delivered, although several have raised the suggestion that car companies—as producers of a technology that alongside burning coal to generate electricity contributes much of the carbon in the atmosphere—should be part of the sweeping solution.

The multi-trillion-dollar global auto industry has found itself smack at the center of what can't be responsibly characterized anymore as a debate. Unfortunately, despite the fact that the majority of car executives aren't global-warming deniers, there are more than a billion vehicles on the roads worldwide, and automakers continue to build millions of new cars and trucks every year. If they stop, or attempt to radically convert to manufacturing vast fleets of Tesla-like vehicles, they'll rapidly go bankrupt.

They are, however, not stupid. Gasoline is simply the most convenient fuel for their products *currently*. Almost without exception, the world's car companies are trying to move themselves in a Teslaesque direction, if haltingly and on a rather small scale at the moment.

Musk bought into Tesla, eventually displacing cofounder Martin Eberhard in an unpleasant management coup, specifically to attack what he considers to be the biggest problem facing humanity. But he didn't want to be boring. He reasoned that a sexy, fast electric car—such as the original Roadster Tesla soon produced—would shake EVs free of their "glorified golf cart" stigma and convince both buyers and investors to fund the demise of the internal-combustion engine.

Tesla began selling stock to the public in 2010, at seventeen dollars per share. A few years later, the Model S was launched; *Motor Trend* would name it Car of the Year in 2013. Tesla had endured numerous near-death experiences prior to the IPO, including an episode in 2008 that brought the company just weeks from bankruptcy. But once the Model S started selling, the accolades began rolling in—the luxurious EV, with its brisk acceleration, sharply minimalist looks, and huge central dashboard touchscreen, was a hit with the automotive media. The stock went, as they say on Wall Street, parabolic; in 2014, it would flirt with $300 per share, ensuring early investors a return of around 1,200 percent.

The financials would pitch and yaw wildly over the next two years, as investors tried to figure out when, if ever, the carmaker would make money and whether its innovations, including an astonishing self-driving autopilot feature, would completely disrupt an auto industry that had been selling largely gas-burning cars, and lots of them, for over a century.

But on that early evening in March, Musk was a conquering hero, a South Africa–born heir apparent to Henry Ford and the late Apple founder and CEO Steve Jobs. Musk's other company, SpaceX, was taking care of another scope of his vision, the effort to make humans a "multi-planetary" species with a colony on Mars, the planet to which Musk said he would retire.

It is easy to understand why Musk, then forty-four, was a model for Robert Downey Jr.'s character Tony Stark in the Iron Man movies. He did cars. He did rockets. He even did solar energy in his role as the chairman of SolarCity, a company started by his cousins. (And acquired by Tesla in 2016 for $2.1 billion.) He was *the* superstar entrepreneur of Silicon Valley. Musk attacked huge problems head-on, like a technologist of old. And he was aware of just how quixotic his ambitions were. Starting a car company, he would say, is idiotic, and an electric-car company is idiocy squared.

What got Detroit's attention that night wasn't the Model 3 itself; the car had been much discussed for several years, and everyone knew what to expect in a smaller, less expensive Tesla. Rather, the star of the show was the preorder counter, displayed behind a bright red Model 3 on a huge screen on the stage.

Analysts had expected something like 150,000 Model 3s to be reserved, each with a $1,000 refundable deposit. By the time I took a photo of the counter at the event, it had crossed 174,000. In a month, 373,000 reservations would be logged, creating the potential for $13 billion to flow into Tesla's needy coffers, assuming a relatively conservative average price of $35,000 for each sale. Who knows how many of those reservations will ultimately turn into sales? Even if only a quarter or a half of them do, it is still an impressive number and a testament to the potential demand.

"So, do you want to see the car?" Musk winkingly asked, before giving three preproduction versions of the car the stage.

A better question—and one that he would ask as the preorders surged—was, "How many of these cars can we actually build?"

The traditional auto industry is secretly obsessed with Tesla. Not since Preston Tucker, an innovator of the 1950s whose quixotic life was chronicled in Francis Ford Coppola's 1988 film *Tucker:*

The Man and His Dream, had anyone so thoroughly captivated the iconic world of the American automobile. The CEOs of major auto companies tend to be either hard-charging, sharp-elbowed "car guys" or technocratic bean counters. Occasionally a major change agent such as Alan Mulally will come along, but many chief executives got to the big chair after decades of loyal service.

When Mark Fields got the CEO job at Ford, he freely admitted that the company had bought a Tesla Model S, taken it apart, and put it back together again. He later said the company would do likewise with the Model X SUV.

But even by the secretive standards of Tesla fascination, the Model 3 preorder palooza was earth-shattering. From Dearborn to Toyota City, the automakers just couldn't believe it. The astounding number of deposits showed the intense desire to join the club that the brand represented. The only meaningful comparison to draw was with Apple. In the auto industry, you could say that Ferrari held a similar mystique, but Ferrari didn't have the ambition to dethrone the gas-burning engine or sell half a million cars a year. Tesla did, and it was sort of appalling to mainstream auto executives.

Traditional automakers work desperately hard to capture and retain customers, spending billions to convince them to stick with certain brands and to advance through vehicle hierarchies, from inexpensive mass-market cars to pricey luxury rides. What was astonishing about Tesla's Model 3 launch was that hundreds of thousands of buyers were happy to give Tesla an open-ended, no-interest cash loan, with no meaningful guarantee beyond Musk's word that the cars would arrive on time. Musk's promises had a poor track record. Both the Model S and the Model X had suffered from production delays and early quality-control problems. In fact, Musk admitted that Tesla had been guilty of "hubris" in designing and engineering the Model X, which had many complicated features that slowed the assembly line. The doors had to be completely redesigned at the eleventh hour. The second-row seats turned out to be so complicated that Tesla would eventually take the supplier off the job and engineer this component itself.

Later, quality-control glitches would appear. The entire Model S fleet was voluntarily recalled in December 2015 because a seat-belt assembly could fail. The initial production run of the Model X, several thousand vehicles, would also be recalled, because third-row seats could pitch forward in a crash. Much earlier, there had been battery fires with the Model S, and Tesla had been compelled to design a shielding system for the bottom of the car to prevent punctures of the battery pack. Tesla's advanced electronics and software, while game changing in many respects, were buggy in the way that Silicon Valley code typically is (the ritual is to release the software and fix it later). In an annual dependability survey by J. D. Power and Associates conducted in 2016, Tesla owners reported so many problems that Tesla finished in the bottom five, undercutting the narrative that its vehicles were redefining the ownership experience with rapid software updates.

Even though Musk admitted that the Model X SUV was so advanced that Tesla "probably shouldn't have built it," his boundless gumption still captivated the industry.

In the traditional auto industry, Musk had only one prominent naysayer, former GM product guru Bob Lutz, who had worked for BMW and for Chrysler under Lee Iacocca before coming to GM and straddling the pre- and post-bankruptcy companies. I talked to Lutz about Tesla on several occasions between 2014 and 2016—once at the Detroit auto show in January 2016, when he was preparing to reveal a new American-made supercar venture with onetime Tesla competitor Henrik Fisker—and he was always unflinchingly equal in his praise for Tesla's cars and his disdain for Musk's management of the company.

Lutz's attitudes toward global warming were controversial. While not exactly a climate-science denier, he was skeptical that taking internal-combustion engines off the road and replacing them with more expensive and less versatile electric cars was a solution. But that wasn't what shaped his negative views of Tesla—he actually didn't think that Tesla was doing a very good job of running its business. In a sense, he and Musk were on the same page: the cars were simply too difficult to build.

But with Ford's and GM's stock prices languishing, even as both carmakers notched steady and impressive profits through 2014 and 2015, executives grumbled about how easy it was for Musk to sell additional Tesla stock, which the carmaker did in both 2015 and 2016, raising almost $2 billion in the process. And even though Detroit had been sweepingly reinvented by the financial crisis, the familiar infighting and territorialism that have always defined the auto industry hadn't disappeared. In the 1980s, Detroit had endured the Japanese arrival in force in the U.S. market. The Big Three had been forced to adapt, to become more efficient, and to see their companies as large manufacturing and management teams, "flat structure" organizations, where the lowliest assembly-line worker had the power to stop production if he spotted a problem. Sure, Toyota and Honda continued to be extremely hierarchical, in the Japanese business tradition. But when it came to actually building cars, the "relentless pursuit of perfection," to borrow a famous tagline from Toyota's Lexus luxury brand, was a mandate that Detroit had to accept. Unsurprisingly, customers preferred cars that always started, didn't rust out in a matter of years, and could be passed down from generation to generation, Dad's Honda Accord becoming Junior's college car.

Musk was a different animal—a leader who called, seemingly, all his own shots. He was initially ridiculed when he appointed himself as Tesla's product architect, while at the same time having an experienced designer, Franz von Holzhausen, from Mazda, for the real aesthetic work, and JB Straubel overseeing how the cars were engineered at the nuts-and-bolts level. But then the Model S arrived, and with it dropped jaws and widespread media accolades.

Musk didn't have to fight through a bureaucracy—he was the bureaucracy, and at Tesla, bureaucracy was the enemy. So if Musk wanted to ignore structure, he just did. He had a hardworking communications team, but if he had something to say, he took to Twitter, often at odd hours and on weekends, sending reporters scrambling. He had hardworking engineers, but if he wanted to make a change to a Tesla vehicle, he made it. In Tesla's required financial filings with the Securities and Exchange Commission, the company never failed to cite the so-called "great man" risk: without Musk, Tesla would be in big trouble. The CEOs of big car companies think they have power, and they do. But Musk had power of a different order, as well as lots of stress.

By the time Ford was turning practice laps at Le Mans in early June 2016, Musk was running a company that was a decade old. And he was under as much pressure to innovate as everyone else in the industry. Ironically, Ford was probably better prepared to manage the transformation in mobility that Tesla was helping to usher in. In the face of a massive disruption to the accepted way of doing business, scale can be an invaluable asset. At base, Musk's company was all about demonstrating that there was a paying buyership for its type of vehicle, reversing the thinking that had followed the demise of GM's EV1 project from the 1990s, which had brought the first mass-produced electric car to market, but only in a limited way, via leasing. When GM decided to conclude the program and crush all the EV1s, save a few historical examples, it was widely assumed that electric cars were once again going to be at best a sideline of the auto industry. (GM's decision inspired the film *Who Killed the Electric Car?* which alleged that the carmaker had acted more to preserve itself from an electric revolution than to dispense with a money-losing experiment.)

Ford's angle on transportation in the twenty-first century was the preoccupation of Bill Ford, who, once Alan Mulally took over as CEO, could concentrate on delivering a deeply counter-intuitive message: that the company we credit with creating the mass-market automobile wanted to curtail its dependence on four wheels and an engine in the future.

The idea was really quite logical. Ford would become a mobility provider. If you needed to own a car, Ford would build one, and Ford dealers would sell it to you—and Ford would lend you the money to buy it. But if you didn't want to own a car, Ford would provide you with transportation. And if you wanted any aspect of your mobility experience to be more pleasant or efficient, Ford would create—or partner with other companies to create—the information corridors to make that happen.

Ford began to tackle this process in earnest around 2010, and Fields made it a prominent part of his leadership pitch once he became CEO. It was a good fit. Fields had always been a forward-looking leader.

Scale can be a strength when a company is being actively disrupted, but the classic theory on the subject—articulated by Harvard Business School's Clayton Christensen in his seminal book *The Innovator's Dilemma*—says that size can protect for only so long. And that's because new entrants can innovate much more rapidly than incumbents, even if the established business is itself actively trying to innovate.

The core problem—an advantage, actually, for smaller, newer companies—is that the very things that insulate the established player prevent it from moving fast enough. The critical sticking point is failure. Big companies can afford to fail, but they can't undertake the failure process rapidly enough. And unless their businesses don't require very much cash for research and development, as is the case with software-driven Internet firms, they can't afford to invest in hundreds of over-the-horizon efforts. For one thing, there's a disincentive for companies that already have scale to do small stuff; it's more cost-effective for them to simply buy up smaller companies. And for another, they can be undermined by competitive threats that are enabled by the newest technologies. It's this second threat that was generating the biggest risks for Ford and its rivals in 2016.

The ride-sharing service Uber, founded in 2009, came on the scene with a brash, sharp-elbowed CEO named Travis Kalanick aiming to eliminate the taxi business in big cities. By the time the Ford GT race cars were getting their first taste of the Circuit de la Sarthe, Uber was valued at a staggering $65 billion and had just taken a $3.5 billion investment from Saudi Arabia's sovereign wealth fund, as the oil-rich nation sought to diversify beyond the natural resource that had transformed it into one of the world's most influential and richest countries.

Tesla shook up the traditional carmakers. But they could still figure out what Tesla was: an automaker with some high-tech credibility and electric motors, plus a charismatic leader. Uber was much harder to figure out. Pundits began to argue that with Uber, nobody—except for Uber drivers—would ever need to own a car again. And as self-driving cars accelerated their development, the drivers started to drop out of the picture. The future would consist of autonomous vehicles, owned as large fleets, appearing and disappearing as needed, dispatched by software.

Design, horsepower, speed, the automobile as an icon of freedom—that would all be relegated to the misty past, like stagecoaches and Conestoga wagons. All that would matter is that your pod-mobile appeared when summoned, and that it moved you from point A to point B.

Automakers were far from sure that this—for them—dystopian future would come to pass, but they were determined to avoid a slide into irrelevance. GM began to move very aggressively in 2015 and 2016, investing $500 million in Uber's competitor Lyft, buying up the assets of a mobility start-up called Sidecar, which had gone bankrupt, and most dramatically, buying an obscure self-driving outfit, Cruise Automation, for nearly $1 billion. By the end of 2016, Cruise's self-driving technology would come to market under the GM banner, as the automaker began selling its Bolt EV, beating Tesla's Model 3 by at least a year.

But Ford wasn't hanging back. It created a small fleet of self-driving cars to perfect the technology, which by 2016 was mainly capable of letting drivers take their hands off the steering wheel for freeway driving, as long as they continued to monitor their vehicles. It was widely expected, however, that over the next decade, higher levels of autonomy would be rolled out, leading ultimately to the end of drivers behind the wheel.

The traditional auto industry is, in fact, pretty good at assessing risks. And the broadly held notion that it just wants to stick to the same old, same old, year after year, is simply false. The industry is far too competitive for anyone to avoid innovation; the carmakers that struggle to sell cars are the ones that are forced to starve their research-and-development budgets for too long. The internal-combustion engine, introduced in the nineteenth century, had been perfected by the early twenty-first, through a process of continuous innovation undertaken by the global auto industry (the gazillion patents related to the internal-combustion engine were one of the reasons that critics often accused the industry of stalling on change). In fact, a few start-ups in the early 2000s and 2010s were even trying to push the internal-combustion engine to breakthrough levels. A company called Transonic Combustion, which failed because it couldn't make its technology adequately reliable, developed a fuel-injection system that upgraded gas-burning efficiency to unheard-of levels, with engines delivering 100 miles per gallon.

By early 2016, Ford felt awfully good about where it stood, in terms of preserving itself and embracing the future. The company even had an in-house futurist on staff, and had since before the financial crisis, to spot important trends before they became existential threats—or massive missed opportunities.

But as someone who had covered the company for a decade, and who had a front-row seat for everything happening in Silicon Valley thanks to my job at *Business Insider*, a website that obsessively monitors, analyzes, and reports on technology, I could tell that the pace of change and the multiplication of risk were picking up speed. Ford had the right overarching idea, as expressed by Bill Ford. It had the right messages, as expressed by Mark Fields. And it had the right people: designers, engineers, and managers who were technologists at heart. Ford even set up shop in Silicon Valley, to be closer to the action.

But this was a global enterprise that employed tens of thousands—and that had to keep its core business cranking. That meant building a million F-150 pickup trucks every year, no small task. Even if 100 percent of the company knew that enormous disruptions were afoot, at best only 10 to 20 percent of the company could focus on Ford disrupting itself.

The scrappy companies that were undertaking the disruption, of course, could go all out on the effort. For them, there was no point in striving to survive—the only acceptable outcome was to make it big, to hit the jackpot, or to vanish completely.

In late 2015, I went to Detroit to interview GM CEO Mary Barra. The first woman to lead a major automaker, Barra said all the right things about how the 100-plus-year-old carmaker, and by association the industry that it was part of, would ride out all the new threats.

At GM headquarters in the Renaissance Center in downtown Detroit, sitting in Barra's large and gracefully appointed but far from ostentatious office, I listened as she accepted the deluge of risk that was sweeping through the industry. Barra had spent her entire life at GM—her father had worked there, and GM was the only place she had ever worked.

"I can't tell you what technology is going to exist in five years," she said. "All I can tell you is that if we sit here five years from today, it will be something that's dramatically impacted the industry that we can't even name right now."

I thought I was being lightly irreverent when I said to Barra that I hoped we could make a date to talk again then. But although she was amused, she wasn't prepared to make light of what she was up against.

"We're going to disrupt ourselves, and we are disrupting ourselves," she said, her voice unwavering after a nearly hour-long interview. "So we're not trying to preserve a model of yesterday."

Ford's Mark Fields unhesitatingly echoed Barra's message. He came to *Business Insider* in March 2016, right before the New York auto show, and in an interview came right out with it. "There's a lot of talk around technology companies disrupting the auto industry," he said. "Our approach is very simple: we're disrupting ourselves." Before the year had ended, he would pledge Ford to get a fully self-driving car on the road by 2021.

To have the CEOs of the two largest U.S. automakers saying exactly the same thing within months of each other might sound like groupthink, but it isn't. The auto industry has been unique not just in declaring a self-disruption and getting out ahead of the curve rhetorically, but in enacting that disruption as enthusiastically as possible, embedding a positive attitude toward new technology in everything it does.

For example, when Fields presided over the reveal of the new GT in early 2015, he stressed how advanced the supercar was—and that it was technology joined to emotion and history. Disruptive technologies made the new GT possible.

And for what it's worth, the GT is the pinnacle of Ford's automotive technology. It is designed to go fast in the straight line and through the corners; crafted almost entirely from carbon fiber, the most advanced material in the carmaker's manufacturing playbook; and powered by one of the most sophisticated engines Ford has ever built, the race-proven, turbocharged EcoBoost V-6. Styled to turn heads, on the street and on the track, it as an emblem, a new icon. Its reveal provided stirring evidence that Ford was back, and better than ever.

But it was also the culmination of a century of one type of thinking about cars. The GT was glorious. But all around it, the idea of a person in a machine going fast—the idea that was the animating spirit of the multi-trillion-dollar global auto industry— was being discarded. In August 2016, Fields announced that Ford would have a small fleet of fully autonomous vehicles on the road by 2021, leapfrogging the more incremental approach to self-driving technology that Tesla and others were embracing. Both the established automakers and the newest of the new entrants anticipated that the driver would exit the stage in the future; at around the same time that Fields made his announcement, Uber rolled out its own driverless test fleet in Pittsburgh.

At one point, a year before the GT hit the floor at the 2015 Detroit auto show, I went on a drive with a company that offered seat time in some of the world's most exotic and exciting cars. I sampled a Lamborghini, a Porsche, a Ferrari, a Maserati, an Aston Martin, and a Mercedes. My partner for the event was a former

Ferrari owner, a young guy who knew and loved high-performance cars. We stopped several times during the day to switch vehicles. At around noon, the gorgeous machines were all lined up in the parking lot of a grocery store in the New Jersey suburbs. My partner had made money when a tech company he was part of was sold. He understood how fast things could change in the new century.

"Look," he said, gesturing toward the supercars, a few million bucks in the best the auto industry had to offer. "We aren't going to see *that* for much longer."

Was he right? I wasn't sure, even though I knew he was without question onto something. Everyone who built and sold cars for a living was trying to figure out what that something would mean. But for twenty-four hours in June 2016, we were going to forget all about disruptions and electric cars and self-driving vehicles and the twilight of the supercars. The best racing teams in the world were headed for a showdown at the toughest race in the world, and I knew I wasn't the only one still excited by the raging machines, at an almost primordial level.

Chapter 10 ≣≣≣

The Road to Le Mans:
Sebring and Long Beach

The Rolex 24 at Daytona had to be forgotten and filed away, but not without Ford Performance and Chip Ganassi Racing learning a couple of important lessons. Multimatic had to sort out the gearbox problems that had doomed the debut in Daytona.

Luckily, they were minor. It was an easy fix—the design of the dual-clutch six-speed was fine, but the durability of the failed actuator valves had to be sorted out. Other problems were just weird: damage to the massive carbon-fiber air diffuser that extends at track level from the GT's rear, underneath the aerodynamic wing; a cut tire on the number 66 that appeared before anyone figured out it was compromised; and some electronic bugs. All of it could be chalked up to a battle plan that didn't survive first contact with the enemy.

Meanwhile, the EcoBoost turbo V-6 looked solid as hell. The full team just had to make sure the drivers could shift gears and that crews wouldn't commit screwups on pit stops.

Everyone also now knew that in competition, the GT was *fast*. This wouldn't necessarily pay off for the U.S. drivers until they got to Le Mans. But for the European team, the 6 Hours of Spa-Francorchamps in Belgium in May, just about a month before Le Mans, would present a good opportunity to show the GTs at their quickest on a big European track with plenty of room to run. Daytona had to be learned from but filed away.

"In racing, it's good to forget," Joey Hand told me. This was hard-won wisdom. Hand was intimately aware of what happens when the brain starts to interfere with the driving. "I've had some big wrecks in my day. If something goes wrong, it's going to hurt. But you're not going to be quick if you're concerned about that."

This is something those who drive fast for a living are surprisingly good at: coming up with pithy words to summarize their way of life. Screenwriters have been giving characters lines like this forever. But somehow, when they come from a real driver, they sound fresh and wise.

Obviously, it isn't just about the person behind the wheel. The car is a major factor. All other things being equal, as the lead-up to Le Mans progressed in late winter and spring of 2016, it became clear that the Ford GT was a car that could do it all. It was fast in a straight line, but it had fantastic handling in the corners—"it turns with braking really well; I can drive it on the brakes," Hand said—and its limits extended beyond the boundaries competing cars could push for.

It was also an easy car to drive. "I jumped right in and felt at home right away," Hand said. "It's not just a badass-looking car." But at base, Hand was a racing realist. "We're the new kids on the block." he said, "We have a lot of people who have done this before. But it's our first time to Le Mans as a group, so we have to do everything right."

After Daytona, which took place at the end of January, the North American GTs would stay in Florida for the 12 Hours of Sebring in mid-March. Then they had two California courses to look forward to: the Long Beach street circuit in mid-April and the Mazda Raceway at Laguna Seca on May 1. These latter two were slower tracks with a lot of turns, where factors such as driving skill, brake durability, and fuel and tire strategy play a bigger role than raw speed.

Daytona had revealed that the car had issues—hardly a surprise, although the gearbox gremlins hadn't shown up during extensive testing prior to the IMSA WeatherTech season kickoff, and other teams in various Le Mans classes were using the Ricardo transmissions that were giving the GT so much trouble.

But the car was also capable of scorching the track, surging straight into the lead pack when everything was properly firing, as Joey Hand had discovered at Daytona, when he was able to confidently mix in with the Porsche 911s and Ferrari 488s until the pit-stop mishap knocked his GT out of the race and off the lead lap. And Ganassi, despite all the problems, was in love with the GT.

"In this series, there's always a new car," he told me. "And with a new car, you look to have one that does what it's supposed to do. And that's what this car does. You make a change and something changes. You're personalizing the car for the drivers and the conditions. Some cars won't let you do that. This car does. It responds well to change, and that's the sign of a good car."

Ford rolled with the punches meted out by the early problems and setbacks and concentrated on getting ready for the remaining races in Florida and California before Le Mans, and on preparing for the European team's April debut at Silverstone in England.

The six drivers Ganassi had ready to strap into their new GTs in Europe were enthusastic about the car, but of course part of getting the job was agreeing to stay on message—they weren't going to complain about a brand-new ride that was under the media microscope as it made its run at Le Mans history.

The U.S. races that followed Daytona gave Ford and Ganassi the chance to sort out the GT's mechanical issues and gave the North American drivers plenty of opportunities to lay down good laps. Sebring was a major improvement over Daytona; the numbers 66 and 67 cars finished eighth and fifth, respectively. It might have gone better for Richard Westbrook and the 67 car but for a slide off the track with only ten minutes remaining on the twelve-hour clock. Up to that point he had been battling for a podium position. The 66 car also ran well, but with Dirk Müller in the seat during a period of rain, the GT hydroplaned in the first turn of the course—which is notorious for its uneven, unpredictable surface—and spent two hours in the garage being patched up. A lucky red flag held the field in the pits, however, while the weather cleared, and by the time Müller, Hand, and Sébastien Bourdais's ride was back on the track, a top ten was still in the cards.

The Ford brass wasn't exactly ecstatic about finishing fifth and eighth, but it was an improvement after Daytona. In his post-race comments, Raj Nair focused on the GT's reliability, which hadn't been a repeat issue. Lingering in the back of his mind, as well, was the GT's speed, which *was* a repeat virtue from Daytona. Ford and Multimatic had built the GT to be fast, aiming to win races from the lead, and in the United States, velocity had been a consistent plus for the cars in their first two races.

The Long Beach race the following month showcased some additional GT capabilities. It could handle well on a tight track. But the racecourse, laid out on city streets, didn't allow the IMSA drivers to totally cut loose and hammer the cars down nice, long straightaways. For that they would have to wait for Le Mans and the Mulsanne, which, if the gearbox issues didn't recur and the drivers could keep the GTs on the track and out of the paddock, could be an ace in the hole for Ford's comeback. But although the gearbox malfunctions weren't a challenge to overcome, racing has a way of throwing up new and often terrifying struggles, always when you least expect it.

The Bubba Burger Sports Car Grand Prix—definitely the oddest race name on the 2016 IMSA schedule—on the nearly two-mile, claustrophobic Long Beach circuit would see Ford Chip Ganassi Racing and driver Richard Westbrook briefly face down a team's and a driver's worst nightmare: fire.

It happened during practice laps on the Friday before the race weekend, when a fuel leak caused an engine fire as Westbrook was getting used to the GT on the legendary, and legendarily bumpy, Long Beach street circuit, which in the late 1970s and early '80s hosted a Formula One race (won by Mario Andretti in 1977). More recently, it has been home to an IndyCar event. A fountain, complete with leaping dolphins, marks the middle of the course.

Westbrook was able to escape his burning GT no worse for wear, but the blaze was disturbing. No sooner had the team gotten a handle on the problems from Daytona, and enjoyed a glitch-free Sebring, than the worst threat imaginable cropped up. Pro drivers are mostly fearless, but they're all terrified, down deep, of suffering the fate of Niki Lauda, the Austrian three-time Formula One champion, who in 1976 crashed at the German Grand Prix, at the Nürburgring track, and was disfigured by fire when he was trapped in his car. (Lauda recovered admirably from the trauma, which sent him into a short coma, by capturing the F1 championship the following year and again in 1984 after coming out of retirement. The Nürburgring remains an important track, but it's no longer used in F1.)

It was ironic that the fire would knock Westbrook's number 67 car out of qualifying, forcing him and his teammates to start at the back of the pack, because just a few days prior to the mishap, in a blog post for Dailysportscar.com, Westbrook had confessed his affection for the Long Beach circuit. "I love street circuits full stop, but Long Beach is a great one," he wrote, before characterizing the tight-quarter racing as "more a case of one eye backwards, one eye forwards, rather than both eyes forwards."

The burned car had to be repaired, and this was where the brotherhood of motorsport, or at least motorsport mechanics, entered the picture: both the Corvette and the Porsche teams offered to help Ford out.

By the time the 100-minute race was ready to start on Saturday, April 16, number 67 was back in action and would just miss out on third place, as Porsche took first, Corvette Racing placed second, and an impressive privateer Ferrari team from Risi Competizione captured third. It was a stunning result for Westbrook's car, which had for all practical purposes been crippled just twenty-four hours earlier. "We fought at the sharp end all race long and finished on the lead lap," he wrote in a blog post. "Daytona we were 30 laps down and nowhere."

Sadly, a malfunction with the number 66 GT's scissor-door hinge doomed it to making up lost laps and ultimately an eighth-place result. By this point, despite their optimism and faith in the GT, the drivers had every right to express frustration and maybe even blame bad luck: gimpy gearboxes, cut tires, a freak fire, spinouts in the rain, and a funky door. But even though they weren't getting the payoff, the cars were running hard and fast. So they had to remind themselves of that, while focusing on the positives.

"I had fun out there," Dirk Müller said after the race, brushing off the door problem with his number 66 car and preferring to dwell on his quick late lap of just under one minute, eighteen seconds. His teammate Ryan Briscoe would argue that the number 67 car, despite starting from the rear, was running so well that it could have nipped Ferrari for a podium opportunity.

Despite the good vibes coming from the drivers, the uneven and by some estimates disappointing results for the North American GT team were leading to considerable speculation that Le Mans in 2016 would be a nice commemoration of the 1966 win for Ford, but probably not an opportunity to drink any Champagne on Sunday afternoon after twenty-four hours of racing. As the end of April neared, the GTs had been pushed around in their racing class by Porsches, Corvettes, BMWs, and Ferraris. The car itself was a hot-looking piece of superlative technology, but it was taking its time serving up much more than a handful of impressive laps. Ominously, none of the races in the United States after Daytona had matched in duration what the GTs would confront in France, and for the European GTs, Le Mans would be the team's first all-day, all-night contest.

What the motorsport pundits and Le Mans veterans had told me before the season started was ringing true. It wasn't that Ford wasn't ready to race, as Dave Pericak had put it several months earlier at the Detroit auto show—it was that Ford simply didn't have enough experience in sports-car competition yet, on the national stage, with cars in this league. Maybe Raj Nair was right, and the retake–Le Mans campaign should have started in 2015. A real possibility of a Ford embarrassment loomed, when what the world had expected back in mid-2015 was a poetic coronation. Panic wasn't really an option, so Ford Performance and Ganassi continued to focus on one race at a time.

And then the GTs' luck started to turn, in a big way and at the best possible time.

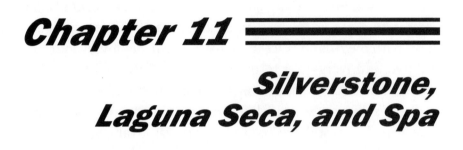

Chapter 11

Silverstone, Laguna Seca, and Spa

The biggest difference between the Ford GT's European and American racing debuts was the climate. Daytona had been an awful outing, but the Florida sunshine was warm and benevolent. The six-hour race at Silverstone took place in mid-April, and the weather was initially looking as if it was not going to cooperate. On April 16, a day before the race, the temperature climbed only into the mid- to high thirties Fahrenheit, and a snowstorm blew through the seventy-year-old venue, about sixty miles north of London in the English Midlands.

That meant difficult conditions and rain tires during qualifying, but the Ford drivers made the best of it, even though one of the two cars endured yet another gearbox issue that limited its shifting to third and fourth gears—fortunately, right in the GT's sweet spot, so that a strong lap time could be recorded. Even with the glitch, Ford qualified in third and fourth positions. Both Pericak and Nair, who were on hand for the European debut, were pleased, although both guys were haunted by memories of the Daytona disaster and the gearbox issues that had destroyed Ford and Ganassi's chances for a headline-grabbing return to big-time sports-car racing.

Just as building both the GT race car and the road car more or less simultaneously, on a time-crunched schedule, initially looked like a colossal undertaking but actually went quite smoothly, the organization of two racing teams, running under different regulations, with the Atlantic Ocean between them, deploying four cars and twelve drivers—not to mention crews for each car—was in practice not that big a deal. Chip Ganassi admitted that there were challenges, but he was quick to note that his people knew what they were doing, and that Ford's support was invaluable. Both the IMSA and the WEC teams were regularly checking in with each other, and of course both Ford and Multimatic had operations in Europe. Bearing the brunt of the struggle to bring four cars to Le Mans was Pericak, who by mid-spring was in full globe-trotting mode, jetting between coasts in the United States, with frequent touchdowns in Detroit, and making jaunts to Europe. Remarkably, the Le Mans campaign wasn't his only job; because he was running all of Ford Performance, he was also overseeing Ford's NASCAR efforts in 2016.

Silverstone turned out to be a decent first outing for the GTs in the World Endurance Championship. The number 67 car, driven by Olivier Pla for the final stint, just missed a podium finish, coming in fourth in a race that was cut short by rain. The number 66 car was close behind, in fifth. Ferrari took the top two spots, and Aston Martin Racing nabbed third.

Competitive themes were emerging on both side of the Atlantic. In the United States, it was Ford struggling to catch up to Corvette as it dealt with the reliability of the GT—a classic confrontation in America, with the Blue Oval taking on a traditional rival in General Motors' Chevy. In Europe, the looming battle was between Ford and Ferrari, a classic in its own right, as it evoked the 1966 Le

Mans showdown. That matchup seemed more logical, given the similar technological natures of the GT and the Ferrari 488, both mid-engine supercars with turbochargers. For the U.S. confrontation, Corvette Racing's wealth of experience was paying off, as the team was coming to the track with a car that had notably less power than the GT.

After Silverstone, the action shifted back to the United States. The Ford-Ganassi team had already moved the operation almost 3,000 miles west, from Florida to Long Beach. Now the team headed for northern California and the Continental Tire Monterey Grand Prix, on the first Sunday in May. The race was a two-hour test.

The Mazda Raceway at Laguna Seca is a two-and-a-quarter-mile track that opened in the 1950s and over the decades has come to be loved by professional drivers and club racers alike. It's a technically challenging course, with eleven turns in total, including the Corkscrew, an incredibly tricky left-right combo that drops 109 feet from top to bottom. That section has made the course legendary; drivers effectively spend an entire lap preparing to tackle it. The beauty of Laguna Seca—which was constructed on a dry lake bend; hence the name—is that it can be driven fast or relatively slowly, by racers of widely varying levels of skill. On balance, however, it's one of those tracks that, on paper, set up better for less powerful cars that are optimized for handling. It's not surprising that it's a favorite of Mazda Miata owners doing "spec" racing of their peppy, low-horsepower roadsters. The Porsche 911 looks, on paper, to be the perfect true race car to bring to Laguna Seca, while the 600-horsepower GT would seem to have too much un-used oomph under the hood.

In 2016, the prototype classes and the GT classes were broken up, so that half of the prototype group ran with half of the GT group; this was required by the limited amount of pit space at the venue. Over the two hours of racing, the fans weren't treated to the usual bonkers straight-line speed of the prototypes, but the racing in the GTLM class, with the Fords battling Ferraris, BMWs, Porsches, and Corvettes, was just about ideal.

The Monterey Peninsula is one of my favorite places on earth, a region of surpassing beauty, with vineyards everywhere, the crashing surf of Big Sur to the south, and the Pebble Beach golf course on the coast. The Laguna Seca race in this environment is a real looker. It's genuinely easy to observe the racing on the track, because the drivers are compelled to do a lot of, well, driving. It isn't necessary for a car to make a lot of pit stops, and with an abundance of turns, there are plenty of chances to work quick passes. The two-hour length of the race is also perfect from a fan's perspective—a sprint rather than a marathon.

The race was excitingly covered on television by Fox, with plenty of cameras inside the cars and around the course. It was like watching hot lap after hot lap, with none of the yawning distance between beginning and end that you confront with Daytona, Le Mans, or even the six-hour races I was familiar with from going to Watkins Glen in upstate New York, another stop on the IMSA sports-car schedule. Watching live racing outside the big oval setups (such as the Daytona 500 and Indy 500) can be like watching a golf tournament. It's hard to tell what's going on, so TV coverage makes for a more educational experience. You see everything important, the big passes and the accidents and mishaps, and you also get some insight in real time from the racing teams.

At the outset of the race, in the GTLM class, Corvette, BMW, and Porsche engaged in considerable dueling—and the Porsches looked sharp, as expected. But Ford and Ferrari were out in front, holding the top three spots. And just over an hour into the race, it started to become clear that Ganassi's strategy was to pit as infrequently as possible, maxing out track time at the risk of running dry on gas and overdoing it with the tires. On a perfectly sunny and dry day, the GTs would wear slicks for the entire race and monitor the degradation of grip closely as the constant turning and drifting chewed away the rubber. One of the quirks of the track is that there's sand everywhere off the paved surface, so the turns can get slippery, and tires can pick up grit if they slide off—grit that can take a few laps to get rid of.

With just over two minutes to go in the race, Richard Westbrook in the number 67 car was pushing the envelope on fuel consumption. With just a single pit stop in two hours, would he be able to get the GT home for the checked flag? He had to pull it off for Ford's first win of the season, as Hand and Müller's number 66 car was too far back to overcome the Ferrari of Scuderia Corsa, a privateer team trailing Westbrook in second.

When Westbrook finally made it across the line, at the North American team's last outing before Le Mans, a page was decisively turned for Ford Chip Ganassi Racing. Both GTs had run immaculately, with no mechanical issues or snafus in the pits. The GTs had qualified in the two and three slots, right behind the Scuderia Corsa 488, which had grabbed the pole. And the EcoBoost V-6 was revealed to be a secret weapon of sorts. Under the hood of a GTLM machine, it could run hard for two hours in the California sun with only a brief break for fuel. This sent a powerful pre–Le Mans signal. In France, you win Le Mans by staying out of the garage and out of the pits.

The entire Ford team was practically giddy. Henry Ford III (briefly misidentified in an on-screen credit by Fox as Ford's "President and CEO," rather than the Performance division's marketing head), Westbrook, and codriver Ryan Briscoe struck a thumbs-up pose for photographers with the Michelin Man mascot (the GTs were running in Michelin racing tires).

Ganassi's engineers were also ready to reveal how they'd come up with their cunning, race-winning strategy. Brad Goldberg told Racer.com that the guys working to get the number 67 car ready in the days before the race had actually *practiced* getting in as many laps as possible without a fuel stop. Racer.com also got a nice scoop on where the whole fuel-saving strategy had originated—at Daytona, remarkably. With the number 67 car knocked out of that race, Briscoe could use his IndyCar, open-wheel racing chops, where fuel strategy is paramount, to give Westbrook ("Westy" to his fellow drivers) a lesson in how to stay off the gas without losing pace or position.

Hilariously, Westbrook got so good at this that by the time the opportunity arose to use his new skills, he executed *too* well. Ganassi's engineers revealed that he had had only enough left in the tank after the race to manage a post-race cool-down lap.

After Laguna Seca, the scene shifted from the baked-brown hills of California to the lush foliage of the Ardennes forest in Belgium, site of the Battle of the Bulge during World War II. Silverstone had given the Ford team confidence, but the 6 Hours of Spa-Francorchamps was a proper preparation for Ford Chip Ganassi Racing's European squad, a test in which the two European GTs would rack up well over 600 miles on the roughly four-and-a-half-mile Spa-Francorchamps circuit before the finish.

It was going to be a tough race by any estimation, on a track that a lot of pros call their favorite. Spa has it all: dramatic elevation changes, huge sweeping turns, tight hairpins, and a long strip of asphalt known as the Kemmel Straight. The circuit is physically spectacular, but as with the Nürburgring in Germany, its history is one of death, mayhem, and carnage. The circuit has been tamed since its grim heyday in the 1960s and '70s, but even with changes that brought Formula One back in 2007, Spa is still deeply respected by drivers. The most harrowing section is the downhill-then-uphill corner called Eau Rouge ("red water," so named because it crosses a stream that has high iron content), perhaps the most admired piece of twisted asphalt in the entirety of motorsport. "If you take away Eau Rouge, you take away the reason why I do this," remarked the late, legendary Ayrton Senna, three-time Formula One champion in the late 1980s and early 1990s.

Eau Rouge has been a controversial section of the circuit for decades, a place where the old attitude of cheating death in very fast machines for fame and glory still holds authentic currency. The corner inspires fear, awe, and desire in equal measure because it has to be taken at high speed to prepare for the long run down the Kemmel. The downhill sweep intensifies acceleration, while the uphill sweep ends blind, so it's difficult to aim for an exit point. The entire sequence is both disorienting and thrilling.

Eau Rouge is where the most harrowing, bad thing yet befell a Ford GT, one that made the gearbox gremlins of Daytona and the freak fire in Long Beach seem like trifling distractions.

Stefan Mücke was at the wheel of the number 66 car, fresh off an engine repair in the pits, when he rounded Spa's first, ultra-tight corner, La Source, and started his run to Eau Rouge and its uphill successor, Raidillon. Mücke was in good form, energized by a duel with his own teammate, the British driver Harry Tincknell in the number 67 car (yes, drivers on the same team will often compete with one another). With about an hour to go, Marino Franchitti had taken over the controls in the 67 GT and was on the lead lap, fighting for a podium spot. Mücke had ground to make up, and he was going to start strong coming out of Eau Rouge.

But the track had other ideas. Afterward, Ford Performance and Ganassi Racing determined that debris on the racecourse had cut Mücke's tire. The result was that the 67 GT spun completely around, screeching, amid plumes of white tire smoke, until first the rear and then the side and front struck a tire wall and were totally shredded. Hanks, hunks, and slabs of the GT's exquisite bodywork were strewn across the track, while a miraculously uninjured Mücke sat inside what was left of his car, and several prototypes dodged the wreckage.

A tense few seconds passed before the crew back in the pits discovered that his radio still worked. "I'm OK," he said. The word was passed to Franchitti, who breathed a sigh of relief, and the safety car was brought out to escort the bunched-up field around the carnage, as crews swept up the remains of the number 66 GT.

Mücke was only bruised and required just a short medical evaluation. The GT had done what a race car is designed to do in a crash—intentionally shatter to absorb the force of the impact and prevent anything deadly from getting to the driver. Nevertheless, the accident was by far the most unnerving and spectacular of the entire sports-car season so far. It instantly reminded everyone not just of Spa's reputation, but that in Ford's campaign to make history, lives were on the line. Far fewer drivers are maimed or killed than in decades past, but even in the twenty-first century, motor racing remains dangerous, and drivers still die at the wheel. And Spa-Francorchamps has been particularly gory. The most infamous incident occurred in 1966, when racing legend—and early advocate for better motorsport safety—Jackie Stewart crashed during a Formula One race and ended up in a farm structure off the course, unable to escape his mangled car while being sprayed with fuel.

The race at Laguna Seca had allowed Ford to leave the United States and head for Le Mans on a high note, exactly as the team had hoped. And although a second-place finish in only the European team's second outing, on a beast of a track, was a fantastic presaging of potential glory on the Circuit de la Sarthe, Mücke's crash meant that one of the four GTs destined for action in south-western France would have to be put back together, if Ford still wanted to take on the legacy of 1966 full force. Strength through speed was Ford-Ganassi's guiding principle, but strength in numbers was a close second.

When I caught up with Dave Pericak after Laguna Seca and Spa, with just over a month to go before Le Mans, he was a changed man from when I had last spoken with him, after the Daytona meltdown. Then, he had almost pledged his considerable reputation on reversing what had gone down in Florida, determined to give the drivers a reliable race car.

"How am I feeling?" he said. "I've finally got some validation that the roller-coaster ride is all worth it. The plan is working, and the team is resilient."

The Laguna Seca win and the second at Spa had obviously given him a second wind, just in time for the big show at Le Mans.

"We need one last push of energy," he said, before conceding that the season was taking a toll. "Our people are tired, man."

Pericak had also gotten plenty of exposure to all the other teams that would be gunning for Ford in the Circuit de la Sarthe. "You can't underestimate anyone," he said. "The competition is the best it's ever been. But now we understand everybody's strengths and weaknesses."

Then he got back to hammering home the message: "We want everybody in our rearview."

The crash at Spa had freaked Pericak out, but he rapidly noted that it had nothing to do with the GT's mechanicals and everything to do with a piece of debris on the track that had killed a tire on one of the wildest turns in racing. "Everybody was concerned," he said. "But once we assessed that Stefan wasn't hurt, we could dig into the data. We were pretty confident that the car was OK, and Michelin looked at everything after the crash."

Pericak's legendary intensity had finally found a more even register, part cheerleader, part engineer, and part student of history.

"We're fortunate to be going back to Le Mans with four cars," he said. But he also knew that for Ford the stakes were only getting higher, with both a win and a solid podium finish on either side of the Atlantic.

"The entire senior leadership will be there," he said. He wasn't kidding, either. Mark Fields, Bill Ford, and Henry Ford III were all going to attend. And Henry III's father, Edsel II, was making his first return trip to Le Mans since he had accompanied his own father, Henry II, in 1966.

I didn't get the sense that Pericak was overly worried or overconfident in this final chat before the team would head for France. Nor did I detect any sense of intimidation. Later, at Ford's paddock hospitality center at the track in France, I would see a guy who was beginning to think that a dream might become reality. He was allowing himself to relax into the possibility of winning, and he was doing this because the technical aspects of the Le Mans campaign had fallen into place. His internal checklist, which he was constantly running and rerunning in his head, was delivering the calm required for him to grin rather than grimace.

Chip Ganassi would be a slightly different story, knowing as he did that he'd never undertaken a Le Mans effort before. It was a remarkable hole in his résumé as a team owner—the second most successful in history, after the older Roger Penske—although he had run the race, in 1987, in a car that failed to finish. Prior to the 2016 season, Ganassi had won virtually everything else with his team, including the Indy 500 and the Daytona 500. This obviously didn't make him cocky. Although he had the best setup an owner could ask for going into Le Mans, as a former pro driver, Ganassi understood that while past results can be a useful guide, a twenty-four-hour race was purpose-built to undermine happy endings.

But Pericak had undergone a modest transformation. A devoted Ford man who had become a minor celebrity thanks to his turn in the Mustang documentary *A Faster Horse*, he had stretched into a new role and become the intensely focused face of Ford's return to endurance racing glory.

There was no doubt about it: Pericak was looking forward to having the Ford brass turn out in force at Le Mans. He was running his own race and making his own bid for history. And although he had been on a rocky ride, by his own admission, the plan that he and his team had created with Ganassi and Multimatic only about 400 days earlier was about to peak.

Destiny was now just over the horizon. The inexorable march of time would carry the GTs to a reckoning. On June 18, the sun would rise over a quiet farming town in southwestern France, where, at the end of a motorway bordered on both sides by waving oceans of wheat destined for the nation's baguettes, the toughest race in the world would happen. The starting grid would form on Saturday, just before three o'clock in the afternoon; the honorary starter would send them off, and by three o'clock Sunday, the world would know whether 2016 would echo 1966. Fifty years later, the scene was the same, more or less. The names had changed, and so had some of the technology, but not enough to alter the simple fact that a car race consists of cars going fast.

Well, most of the names had changed. At least two were the same, separated by half a century and several generations: Ferrari and Ford.

Chapter 12

You Want to Win the Big Ones

In 1966, the only way to prepare for Le Mans was to have run it in the past or to arrive the week before to get in some practice laps, if you had never sampled the Circuit de la Sarthe in the flesh. This gave Le Mans a mysterious and somewhat unknowable quality—for almost the entire year, the course gave itself back to the citizens of France, who would drive at normal velocity down the Mulsanne Straight and never be forced to negotiate the Porsche Curves. Consider that: the racecourse with the fastest average speed in the world is, for much of the year, a cluster of downright boring, sleepy thoroughfares. You might see a truck. You might see a tractor. You might see somebody with a Ferrari—on vacation.

Numerous members of the Ford Chip Ganassi Racing team had Le Mans experience, but they wanted to tune up before the main event in June. This is where twenty-first-century technology gave them a leg up on the 1966 drivers. In 1966, Bruce McLaren and Chris Amon and their teammates had a GT40 to turn laps in; in 2016, Joey Hand and Ryan Briscoe had a full-on simulation of their Le Mans–bound GT car at Ford's Performance Technical Center in North Carolina. What a difference five decades make.

The simulator was first activated in 2014, about two years before the 2016 Le Mans, and it's used by Ford NASCAR drivers as well as the sports-car racing teams. Located in a 33,000-square-foot facility devoted exclusively to racing training and preparation, the simulator consists of a driver's compartment that's actuated by a computer-controlled system that can generate exceptionally realistic racing conditions. From the cockpit, the driver looks out at a vast curving screen whose images are delivered by five projectors.

"It's an immersive experience," Hand said, in a Ford Performance video released before Le Mans. "It's as real as you can get. You're trying to put the lap down. You're huffing and puffing. You're sweating."

Beyond giving the drivers a chance to experiment with the unique performance characteristics of their car on the tracks they'll actually be competing on, one of the key advantages of the simulator is its capacity to allow the team to play around with different vehicle setups and to discern which ones blend best with the skill of the driver, the technology of the car, and the peculiarities of a given track.

Raj Nair loved it. "It will help us push handling to the next level, so that our cars can be fast right off the trailer," he said. He also liked that when the real-life cars couldn't turn laps, the simulator could be used to make additional setup changes between practice sessions and race day. It was the ultimate preparation machine.

The Ford-Ganassi drivers needed all the preparation they could get, because even though some had Le Mans experience, the Circuit de la Sarthe is a racing anomaly, requiring a different competitive metabolism from what the Ford team had brought to other events. The truly tricky thing is that it's possible to lapse into and out of full concentration at Le Mans, thanks to the Mulsanne.

This gives the drivers a way to gather themselves on every lap, to simply put the hammer down and let the car fly. But it also means that they have to snap back into aggressive driving mode for the remainder of the lap.

The Circuit de la Sarthe is essentially composed of three sections. The long Mulsanne Straight is in the middle. Preceding it is the escape from the grandstand and pits area and the sharp right-hand Tertre Rouge corner leading to the straightaway. Then, the slam-on-the-brakes hairpin at the end of the Mulsanne sets up a sequence of turns—Indianapolis, Arnage, the Porsche Curves, and the Ford Chicanes—before the cars reenter the stands complex and start all over again. There isn't much in the way of elevation change, so a great Le Mans lap boils down to setting a pace on the Mulsanne, then finding a good line through the curves, with a car that has an aerodynamic package that's set up for straight-line speed, not to deliver strong downforce in turning.

In the twenty-four hours, the drivers will navigate the circuit well over 300 times, racking up nearly 3,000 miles in the process—a trip from Paris to Istanbul and back.

But Le Mans isn't just twenty-four hours of turn, let 'er rip, turn-turn-turn, repeat. There are sixty other cars on the circuit. Drivers in the GTE Pro class have to contend not only with the prototype-class field made up of much faster cars, but also with GTE Am machines that are slower. Traffic issues, especially during the early stages of the race, should not be underestimated.

For all the cars in the GTE Pro class, there will also be a potentially endless series of tweaks and adjustments once the race is under way. Practice and qualifying can give a team a good sense of what's working and what isn't. Have we adjusted the angle of the rear wing correctly to provide enough downforce to keep the car solid in the corners but not make it slow on the straights?

Are we comfortable with the tire compounds we want to use? Of course, the race itself always throws up new challenges and forces the team to ask itself dozens of unanticipated questions.

"The important thing is to have a plan," Chip Ganassi told me on the day before the race. "The other thing to do is to be able to change your plan."

Rain means tire changes, but dry doesn't mean that only one type of tire will be used; a team might put different tire compounds on to enhance speed or handling. The aerodynamics may have to be adjusted. A driver may have to push hard if he falls off the pace, affecting the fuel strategy. Electronic glitches can show up. And that's just the routine stuff. All bets are off if the car is damaged in a minor mishap, as Ford learned at Daytona, when a broken rear diffuser ended up shredding a tire before anyone noticed that it was a problem.

Of all the teams converging on Le Mans in June, Ford's had the least preparation for this intricate, exhausting undertaking. The first prototype GT race car had been rolled out only thirteen months earlier. There had been precious few testing opportunities on the track—known as "shakedowns"—prior to Daytona, so Ganassi and his drivers were still learning the car. Only Ferrari was in a similar boat. Corvette, Porsche, and Aston Martin were all running proven cars. And over the course of four races in the United States and now two in Europe, the competition in the GT classes had been fierce. It had been the best season for sports-car racing in years, a thriller for the fans but commensurately nerve-racking for the drivers and teams.

The guys who would don the helmets for Ford-Ganassi were holding up best; the ups and downs of racing were familiar to them, and like most pro athletes they found value in evening out their highs and lows, fully cognizant that as sports-car drivers, they were running not just small marathons in individual races but a yearlong stretch that would determine whether they had done their jobs.

On the executive front, Dave Pericak's intense, hypercompetitive nature and devotion to the Blue Oval were taking a toll, but he was closing in on the big prize. When I saw him the day before the official start of the 24 Hours of Le Mans, he reminded me that, win or lose, Ford still had a full IMSA/WEC season to complete. But Ford hadn't built a new GT to take an IMSA or WEC crown, and Le Mans was not just another race on the schedule. If sports-car trophies were all Ford wanted to bring back to Dearborn, the carmaker didn't have to design and build an entirely new car and expose itself to the risks and embarrassments it had already faced.

Raj Nair meandered over to join us. He was mellower and more cheerful than Pericak, but he was also hedging. Pericak was on a mission, but Nair was a pragmatist. He knew that Ford had implicitly over-promised with a new GT and the Le Mans return, and he was prepared to under-deliver. He had also found out the hard way that although the GT program had come together almost flawlessly in 2015, the 2016 racing season had really kicked the car and the team around. Nair was about the same size as Pericak—neither was a big guy—but he was dressed in more monochromatic clothes, mostly dark blue. Pericak had on his blindingly white Ford Performance polo shirt. Nair was his usual funny self, down deep a Midwestern kid who loved cars and was living a dream at Ford, but also a tad evasive, reluctant to make eye contact when I brought up the abandoned Mustang plan. Pericak had the ability to stare right through you, so concentrated was his intensity. The first few times I experienced it, I found the stare unnerving. But I quickly realized that Pericak was a true-believer type who also happened to have a generous heart . . .

Nair was more diplomat than soldier, an important foil to Pericak's battlefield commander. It wasn't easy to discern what Nair
really thought. But there was no question that he was constantly
assessing the odds, like a good engineer, and—like a good business
leader—trying to figure out how to deal with numerous contin-
gencies. He and Pericak made an interesting pair.

If Pericak was determined, and Nair diffident, then Chip Ganassi
was a weathered realist who wasn't required to serve up any messages about Ford's run at history. In person, Ganassi was taciturn
and borderline gruff, but as soon as you thought he wasn't even
remotely interested in answering your questions, he would loosen
up and engage in a little freestyle speculation on the GT's chances,
or the team's performance prior to Le Mans, or the whole mad
adventure that was motorsports.

The curious thing about Ganassi was that although he had been
a successful driver, he didn't act much like a driver anymore. That
peering-into-the-future driver stare didn't appear in his eyes. He
also didn't make promises or call his shots. After I had been following the GT and its return to Le Mans for a year, it struck me
that Ganassi was the critical player in the drama who *least* yearned
to win the race. And that was reassuring. It meant that as the
thousands of decisions piled up from January to June, he would
be able to handle the pressure and manage the overload. Winning
wasn't an endgame for Ganassi—it was simply the result of proper
planning and solid execution. The right drivers plus the right car
plus the right strategy—plus a bit of luck—would bring the likeli-
hood of a Le Mans victory into view. Then it was just a matter of
pushing to that next level.

Le Mans is not a commitment to be taken lightly. The race con-
sumes an entire week, and it happens in the fairly remote countryside southwest of Paris. Literally right next to the track section

and stands there's an airfield, home to the famous Dunlop Bridge that drivers pass under as they begin a lap around the Circuit de la Sarthe. So if you have a private jet, a personal airplane, or access to a helicopter, you can zip right down from the City of Light. For kicks, I investigated a charter chopper, recalling that that's how Henry Ford II commuted to Le Mans in 1966. The estimate was about five grand for the ride.

It requires two trains to make the trip from Paris, so I decided to rent a car. My Renault Captur, a small diesel SUV, was both my chariot and my bedroom (for a night), and the car and I enjoyed our two-hour drive down and back, predominantly on the A11 motorway, which rolls past Versailles and Chartres and through the vast wheat fields of France's breadbasket.

Because I was just there to watch the race and talk with Ford's executives and the Ganassi drivers and team members, I had it relatively easy. The competitors, however, while negotiating their way into and out of the facilities, trying to get used to the cars and the circuit, would be compelled to participate in the many festivities and local customs and traditions that have evolved over almost a century's-worth of annual twenty-four-hour races.

When I'm asked to describe Le Mans, I usually say it's the Burning Man of motorsports. It has that flavor of a mass of people who are passionate, even obsessive, about something, gathering in an obscure corner of the world and staying awake all night, while various musical acts perform and everyone waits for an exciting, climactic event. But on a more mundane level, Le Mans is sort of like a mass camping trip with a car race in the middle. There's even a small carnival, complete with a full-size Ferris wheel.

Ford CEO Mark Fields was on his second trip to Le Mans when I caught up with him on Saturday. He was really into the whole crazy scene. "You won't believe what I saw when we were driving in this morning," he said, excitedly. "An Aston Martin—parked next to a pup tent! A pup tent! I took a picture."

That is Le Mans. I myself saw a $300,000 orange McLaren supercar parked next to a camper—and took a picture. There were Porsches everywhere, and next to those Porsches were tents. Ford and Ford owners had brought a massive contingent of the previous-generation, mid-2000s vintage GTs, along with lots and lots of Mustangs. On the drive back to Paris after the race, I was passed by a line of three Ferraris.

All the tents and campers and mobile homes and temporary shelters, some large enough to house big-screen TVs and requiring portable generators, are actually sensible. Hotels in and around Le Mans are booked up well in advance, and there aren't that many of them to begin with. And if you are staying off-site, traffic can be horrible getting into and out of the parking areas. Once I was in, I decided I was in for the long haul—forty-eight hours in total, from Friday to Sunday. It was plenty of fun. On the first night, a group of boisterous young Frenchmen who had parked their pickup truck behind my car were both drinking heavily and preparing to cook some food on a small charcoal grill. When I told them I was from the United States, their apparent leader asked me why I was driving a shit car like the Renault and then expressed his undying devotion to Cadillac. So strong was his devotion that he had the Cadillac shield tattooed in full color across his chest, with an American eagle perched on top; in the talons of one foot the eagle held Arnold Schwarzenegger's machine gun from the movie *Commando*, and in the other, Sylvester Stallone's serrated survival knife from *Rambo*.

"I love America," he said, and given what I had already seen, that sounded like an understatement.

"America! Fuck, yeah!" his chorus of compatriots added. That sounded like an understatement, too. We discussed all things Yank for several minutes before I ducked inside my Renault for a few hours of sleep.

Le Mans builds to its conclusion, and the building began several days before the Saturday start. It's a bit like a prizefight. The teams have to subject their cars to a technical assessment by the Automobile Club de l'Ouest (ACO), called "scrutineering," on the Sunday and Monday of the week before. If they pass, they can turn practice laps and go through eight hours of qualifying on Wednesday and Thursday. Qualifying involves at least two drivers from each three-man team completing at least one timed lap in a twenty-minute run around the circuit, according to FIA/WEC regulations. The circuit is so long that numerous cars can be qualifying at the same time. If a car can't complete its run—owing to mechanical failure—then it won't qualify. The two best lap times for each driver are averaged to establish a "reference time," and the fastest reference time wins the pole. Everyone else lines up sequentially behind that car. It all wraps up with a traditional drivers' parade on Friday.

Meanwhile, hundreds of thousands of hard-core racing fans, day-trippers, and those exhibiting merely idle curiosity about a race that runs for an entire day drifted into and out of the venue. Apart from the sprawling campgrounds, the semipermanent areas around Le Mans provided abundant distractions. There's an entire Le Mans museum chronicling the multiple decades of the race. There's also what's referred to as a *village*, which is really more of a food court—serving an immense amount of beer. The village is mixed with a shopping mall, complete with a Rolex shop in the middle and, in 2016, a jumbo screen broadcasting the European Cup soccer tournament. Scattered around are the food trucks, where you can get your crêpes filled with Nutella or spiked with Grand Marnier.

The manufacturers erect immense hospitality facilities, exclusive two-level temples from which friends and family can get a good view of the cars as they exit the Mulsanne Straight and make their runs through the turn complexes and back to the stands and the pits and paddock. Some of the automakers—Audi, Porsche—that have won Le Mans and come back every year, competing in multiple classes, occupy huge, permanent structures festooned with their brand logos. There they host elaborate multicourse dinners before, during, and after the race, and loyalists can grab a drink, a snack, or a coffee at all hours when the twenty-four-hour clock is officially ticking down.

For the media the amenities weren't quite as lavish. The publishers of the Michelin Guide series, the renowned evaluator of the world's finest restaurants, set up a lounge directly above pit row and kept the wine, beer, and Champagne flowing, along with restorative coffees. Deep into the night on Saturday and Sunday morning, servings of rillettes, the tasty pâté-like spread that's the signature dish of the region, were set out. It was all quite civilized, a contrast with some of the staggering drunkenness on display outside the stands; at one point, I saw a gentlemen with a head wound, covered in dried mud from what I assumed was a fall, ordering yet another beer at one of the many bars in the village section, then wobbling off in search of joy and mayhem. Le Mans is a twenty-four-hour party, stretched out to forty-eight or even seventy-two, depending on your stamina, enthusiasm, and willingness to rough it in the French countryside.

But the racing teams were worried that the actual race was going to be anything but festive. There was a good chance that lousy weather would make conditions difficult. In the weeks leading up to Le Mans, France had been hit with biblical rains. In Paris, the Seine had overflowed its banks, and the Louvre had been forced to close and move 7,000 artworks to higher floors. The forecast for the Le Mans weekend predicted a deluge sometime after the start on Saturday, followed by clearing and sunshine on Sunday. It often rains for Le Mans, but the timing of the wet is everything. Early rains can disadvantage the faster cars, preventing them from establishing an early lead. The field gets bunched up, as the heavier GT cars mix in with the prototypes, sometimes taking the most powerful and exotic Le Mans machines out of their front-running status. Rain at night means the track will take longer to dry out, preventing teams from getting off wet tires and back onto racing slicks, another disadvantage for the faster cars. And rain during practice and qualifying can both limit performance and curtail the drivers' critical preparation of themselves for the circuit.

When I asked Joey Hand on Friday about the weather forecast, he said the right thing—that Le Mans is Le Mans, and you have to work with what you're given. But he also knew that the GTs were running better in dry conditions, and he admitted that the team would prefer it if most of the race were dry. I neglected to ask him whether the Ford simulator in North Carolina could realistically represent a soggy Circuit de la Sarthe.

By Friday, however, Ford's biggest challenge wasn't Mother Nature. The problem was that the GTs had improved their lap times around the Circuit de la Sarthe by far more than the race organizers had expected.

At the beginning of June, it had been the Corvettes that turned the fastest laps. A GTE Pro–class car can get around the circuit in less than four minutes, and both Corvettes entries did it in 3:55. The GTs weren't as quick, but when official qualifying rolled around in the week before the race, the situation had been reversed. Now the GTs were the fastest cars in the field over the two-round qualifying period, while the Vettes were the *slowest*.

The Corvettes weren't too far off their practice-week pace of 3:55 (they would never add a full second, reaching 3:56). But both the GTs and the new Ferrari 488 blitzed the circuit at pace no slower than 3:52—and one car, the number 68 GT, nearly broke 3:51.

In sports-car racing, the governing authorities don't want one type of car design or engine configuration to run away with a race. They also don't want the gaps between classes to get too small or too great. So during qualifying, the ACO kept track of who was fast, who was slower, and why. It did this during practice, and it also took into account previous performance in races. Then the overseers of competitive fairness determined whether "balance of performance," or BOP, adjustments would be required of the teams, based on a formula that is developed by analysis of the data.

BOP adjustments had already been ordered for the Corvettes, after testing a week before Le Mans qualifying had revealed what the ACO decided was excessive speed. But were the adjustments too much? In qualifying, the Vettes were four and a half seconds slower around the circuit than the quicker Ford GTs.

Most of the GTE Pro field fell in for BOP tweaks before Saturday, and for most of Friday afternoon, a controversy bubbled up, threatening to tarnish Ford's assault on history. All four GTs were *very fast* in qualifying, with the number 68 car taking the pole position. The Ferraris were also quick, but the Corvettes and Aston Martins were unexpectedly slow. The Porsches had been hit with the same BOP adjustments as Corvette during testing.

This meant that the ACO was going to compel Ford and Ferrari to make changes, while Corvette, Porsche, and Aston Martin would be allowed to set their cars up for more speed. The core problem was the variety of machines running in GTE Pro. Ford and Ferrari had low-slung supercars, the Fords using the 600-horsepower EcoBoost twin-turbo V-6 engine and the Prancing Stallion teams saddling up the new 606-horsepower twin-turbo V-8.

Aston Martin had a big 480-horsepower V-8 under the hood, up front. Corvette had a potent V-8, also up front. Porsche had its famous Boxster six-cylinder power plant, but it was located over the rear-drive wheels. Porsche's aerodynamic design, when you got right down to it, dated to the 1960s, when the rear-engine Porsche 911 had first appeared. It was among the most durable and effective sports-car designs ever, but both Ford and Ferrari were using state-of-the-art, twenty-first-century aerodynamics, with the bodywork on the GT and the 488 adding to the downforce. Corvette's design for the C7.R was relatively new, and while the Aston's styling was longer in the tooth, it was contemporary.

The grumbling over the BOP situation reached its loudest pitch toward nightfall on Friday, June 17. The ACO would have to decide by the end of the day whether to assess penalties. In the media center, there were mutterings that Ford had played chicken with the racing authorities and up until Friday had gotten away with it. The accusations cut both ways. There were rumors that the ACO wanted to pit Ford against Ferrari, to put a sharp point on the revival of the 1966 contest. But Ford's Raj Nair suggested that some competitors—not Ferrari—had held back in qualifying. Dave Pericak told reporters at Le Mans that the suddenly slow Vettes were suspicious.

There wasn't anything on trial here besides good sportsmanship. It wasn't against the rules to run slower prerace laps, but it wasn't in the spirit of the competition. Teams were supposed to show what they had, turning laps as close as possible to what they would generate at race time.

After discussions, the ACO instructed Ford to reduce the turbo boost that its engines were producing. Both Ford and Ferrari were also ordered to add weight to their cars—twenty-two and thirty-three pounds, respectively. Corvette, Porsche, and Aston were allowed to adjust a technology called a restrictor plate to permit their uncompressed-air-breathing, non-turbo motors to inhale more oxygen. And Ferrari and Corvette were given a tiny bump in the amount of fuel they would be permitted to use (at Le Mans, fuel strategy is essential, because teams don't have an unlimited quantity). Obviously, with the ACO and the teams meeting to go over the BOP issues on Friday night, it would be impossible to figure out before the race began whether the field had been aligned. The next time the GTE Pro cars took to the circuit, they'd be warming up to race for real. Porsche's head of motorsports, Frank-Steffen Walliser, was profoundly upset and complained emotively about the BOP. Some reporters said he was practically in tears.

But that wasn't the end of it, because anytime there's a BOP controversy, there's talk of gamesmanship. Ford was swiftly accused of sandbagging—initially holding back on lap times, then letting it rip when it came to qualifying. With that strategy, there would be no BOP issues until it was too late to deny the quick GTs the pole, as well as another three good starting spots on the grid.

This didn't make much sense to me, given that such a move would have brought the at-times unpleasant internal politics of motorsports into the picture and tarnished Ford's run for glory. However, I did wonder whether in the two European races leading up to Le Mans, the GTs had been held back, not showing their true potential until Le Mans loomed. I knew, after all, that on the fast Daytona track, when the GTs were healthy, they turned in blistering lap times. It also stood to reason that the lightweight GTs, making 100 more units of horsepower than the Vettes, should be smoking fast, particularly on the Mulsanne.

Besides, it appeared that everyone was fooling around a bit. Ford couldn't understand why Corvette was so slow and said as much. The Ferraris, which had been setting the track on fire in Europe up to Le Mans and were considered by Ford's drivers to be very quick, were abruptly slower than the GTs. For its part, Porsche appeared to be making the best of a difficult situation while hoping for enough rain to slow everybody else down.

Balance of performance itself was coming under criticism. The leveling-of-fields approach is controversial. It makes for technically tighter racing, but it also bunches up fields and creates the potential for crashes. Then there was the obvious question of why the ACO would allow so many different kinds of cars and engines into GTE Pro—and then hold back the faster cars. A more staggered race would be the outcome, presumably with the Fords and Ferraris out in front, followed by Corvettes and Porsches, which switch off positions, depending on whether they are negotiating the Mulsanne or the curves that follow.

In the end, the teams took it all in stride, and the controversy didn't overshadow the race. We'd later learn that the BOP changes were probably justified—and hadn't hurt anyone's chances (although I certainly heard complaints, even months after the race was over). But it all made for a tense sideshow as Friday drew to a close.

Qualifying had gone well for Ford, the BOP controversy notwithstanding. The number 68 car took the pole for GTE Pro, after Dirk Müller turned in a 3:51 lap on Wednesday night. Lousy weather on Thursday kept anyone from besting Müller's time. The other three GTs, numbers 69, 67, and 66, were close behind, in the second, fourth, and fifth positions, respectively.

The number 68 GT's qualifying run had been hairy until the tail end, when Müller had only fifteen minutes in which to manage an impressive lap; his fellow drivers, Joey Hand and Sébastien Bourdais, had been challenged by traffic issues, as the German driver later recounted.

"The car felt really good," Müller said, although he admitted that he, too, was struggling with traffic. But then his team manager offered words of encouragement—on the radio—and Müller buckled down. "It was a cool lap."

Throughout Friday there was palpable tension in the Ford camp that had nothing to do with BOP. Adjacent to the very cozy paddock at Le Mans, Ford had a lounge and hospitality area for drivers, executives, race-team members, and guests, including members of the media. It was two stories of Ford blue, with catered food and a coffee bar, plus plenty of monitors on which to watch the race and keep track of the GTs' positions. A short walk away, adjacent to the track, Ford had erected an altogether more ostentatious hospitality structure, also two stories, with an outdoor viewing balcony, several bars, and again plenty of monitors. It was a substantial step up from Daytona, where Ford hospitality had been just a row of tents, and it showed how committed the automaker was to its Le Mans comeback.

Ganassi, the drivers, and both Pericak and Nair were hanging around, attending to a run of press events that the ACO had scheduled. You could tell that they were all trying to relax—trying to *force* themselves to relax. For the drivers, training had kicked in. They knew how to chill. For Ganassi, experience was key. He knew how to put on a game face before a big race. The Ford brass also tried to keep the mood low-key. Winning wasn't a demand in this environment.

But the weight of the moment was heavy. The sensible effort that everyone was making to remain calm was exerting its own kind of strange force. I could feel it. It wasn't a sense of pressure. It was more a sense of dawning realization: *We could actually do this. We could win Le Mans fifty years after Ford's greatest racing triumph ever.*

Joey Hand called it "anxiousness"—not nervousness. Everyone just wanted to get out and start racing; they all wanted to begin to do what they came to do.

The glitches with the cars had been addressed. The GTs had set a blistering pace. The drivers that made up the individual teams for each of the four cars now knew one another well and had forged bonds of camaraderie in the cockpit. The crews were seasoned, after a total of six races on two continents. By Friday morning, you also knew that Ganassi had a game plan, and that he could quit sweating his strategy.

The weather was good. A misty dawn was followed by a beautiful morning: cool but sunny, with low gray-white clouds scattered through a thin blue sky. Conditions were mostly dry, although there was a lot of mud and standing water in the parking areas and campgrounds. Rain was expected toward nightfall, but the morning and early afternoon on Saturday would be dry. A perfect start was in the cards. By nine a.m., the stands were already beginning to fill in with fans jockeying for spots. Outside the stands, a thousand camp chairs were being unfolded and positioned on knolls and hillocks and close to fences. The revelers of the previous night shuffled around in their small backpacking tents and started to prepare for another full day and night of pleasure. The guy with the Cadillac tattoo and his mates gathered up their gear and changed into fresh clothes.

The eighty-fourth installment of the 24 Hours of Le Mans would commence by mid-afternoon. Casual fans were completely psyched. They'd picked up on the GT story and were eagerly anticipating Le Mans, but some were still coming to grips with how patchy the first Ford IMSA/WEC racing season had been. Motorsport junkies were a bit more jaded. The pole was a good sign. But it was also symbolic.

Chip Ganassi was the least impressed of all. "Am I happy to have the pole?" he asked, rhetorically. "Sure, you're happy to have the pole."

It was vintage Ganassi. We were sitting across from each other in the Ford paddock unit, drinking coffee. The race would start in just over twenty-four hours. But he wasn't going to go out on any limbs.

"But in terms of competitiveness, the pole doesn't mean anything," he added, with a slight grin. "It's great, it's a nice PR thing. It looks great as a headline going into the race."

But Ganassi was clearly pleased to have a quartet of cars to work with. "If you have one car, you have one strategy. I don't know what your chances are of doing well with one car, but with four cars, they're at least four times better."

What he meant was that with one car, a team can tackle the race from only a single angle. Maybe they run fast; maybe they hang back. To avoid wrecking the car, they hold off on making any big moves until the sun rises and the race has only a few hours left. Regardless of what they choose, they come up with a plan and are bound by it.

Ganassi had a lot more options. He could run two GTs hard and hold two back, or he could unleash them all. He could send one out fast and make the field chase it, trying to break down a few competitors at the expense of one of his four cars. Or he could use two cars to do that and break down more competitors. He could box in another car and make its hapless driver overextend himself trying to get out. The list of possibilities went on and on. With four cars, Ganassi had more choices than any other team captain in the GTE Pro class.

The grid wasn't formed until just before race time, and the start was vastly different from that of 1966. For one thing, a Ford family member didn't wave the French flag to send the drivers off, as Henry II had in 1966. A sleekly attired Brad Pitt, in smoky sunglasses and a slick, artful haircut, did. There also wasn't a "Le Mans start." In 1966, the drivers had to run to their cars at the start, firing them up and rocketing off from pit lane without even strapping in first. This ended in 1969. In 2016, the field was led around by a safety car, until the green flag dropped and true racing could be unleashed.

But before all that, there were more rituals. Two hours before race time, the cars moved into position, pushed by their crews, with the prototypes in the lead. It was an impressive sight, the colorful liveries polished to a high gloss, a wild tapestry of colors spread out beneath the spectators in the stands: in GTE Pro, the Fords were in the all-American red-white-and-blue, while the Ferraris, of course, were *rosso corsa*, racing red, and the Corvettes were a lurid yellow. Huge sponsor logos occupied the background, those of well-known global icons like Dunlop, Porsche, and Rolex alongside obscure French brands unknown to the international audience watching the race on TV and the Internet.

Bibendum, known as "Bib"—the Michelin Man, in English—bobbed along the grid. He was a very French mascot, adorable, and not nearly as tall as I had expected.

Then came the national anthems of the nations that were participating, highlighted by Brits singing along enthusiastically to "God Save the Queen." When the "Star-Spangled Banner" was played, I scanned the stands for Americans doing the American thing, hats off and a hand on the heart, but I didn't spot any. Many, of course, were down at the Ford hospitality tent, out of my view.

An hour before race time, flag bearers—mostly young women in snug cream dresses, pink scarves, and high black stiletto heels—stationed themselves around the starting grid. So French. I wondered how a team feels about its chances if it has a man, not a woman, holding its national flag.

Ominously, with the final hour before the start ticking down, the skies darkened and storm clouds moved in, ahead of schedule. The rain started to fall just as the "Marseillaise" was struck up. The women in the white dresses were attended to by a squadron of umbrella wranglers. A French military helicopter buzzed the stadium at 2:15.

The cars were fired up, but already there was trouble for Ford. The number 67 GT was rolled off the grid and back into the garage. Pericak told me that it was his only moment of real terror.

Was it an isolated problem, or were all four cars beset by the same fault? Yet again, it was a gearbox issue, but the other three cars weren't affected. Ford-Ganassi's strength-in-numbers strategy was already challenged—and an official lap had yet to be turned.

During warm-up laps, the cars started to throw up modest rooster tails of spray. They were all running slicks, but as the rain intensified, each slipped back into its starting-grid spot and the crews came out with rain tires on rolling racks and speed wrenches hooked up to air compressors on carts.

The number 67 GT was still in the garage. The crews calmly made the change from slicks to rain tires, but the grid was chaotic, a blur of activity. The sixty cars tied the record for the size of the field. Officials, photographers, and the now-damp flag bearers were mixed in with helmeted pit-crew members in fireproof racing suits. The Patrouille de France, the precision team of the French air force, ripped across the sullen sky, the eight jets in a tight V formation, trailing plumes in the blue, red, and white of the French tricolor, only to have them rapidly blurred by the rain.

At three o'clock precisely, the din of five dozen high-performance machines being brought to roaring life at once cut through what had become a downpour. Millions of dollars of primo racing technology was getting drenched. The headlights came on, white for the prototypes, yellow for the GT cars. Windshield wipers were activated.

"It rattles your teeth to be on the grid," Brad Pitt said afterward, with the reverence that Le Mans often and unexpectedly brings out.

The true teeth rattling had to wait for a while, however. The start was awkward and slow, and it still lacked the number 67 Ford GT. The safety car led a sluggish, soggy procession around the Circuit de la Sarthe, with laps being counted off at a pace drastically below what kicked in once the race officials determined that the course was safe enough for flat-out racing. These machines weren't designed to go thirty miles per hour.

It took nearly an hour for the officials to make their determination. Race marshals were literally on the circuit with brooms sweeping away the puddles in the curves and corners as the field turned agonizingly poky laps behind the Audi safety car. The number 67 GT, gearbox repaired, left the garage at last, but it was already two laps down. When the safety car finally peeled off, the 2016 24 Hours of Le Mans had become the *23* Hours of Le Mans.

Chapter 13

We're Going to Win from the Lead

The immediate battle among the prototypes consumed everyone's early attention. Prototypes can turn laps thirty seconds faster than the GT cars, so it wasn't long before they pulled away and some gaps opened up. Dirk Müller made good on the pole position and led the GTE Pro class in the number 68 Ford GT. His first fast lap in the wet was 4:23, much slower than in the qualifying run. Olivier Pla and Richard Westbrook trailed in the numbers 66 and 69 cars. The Fords were mixed in with the Ferraris and Porsches. The number 67 car was out of it, but with a mountain of time for the field to climb before Sunday afternoon, anything was possible.

By 5:30, a pattern had emerged that defined the race for the GTE Pro class. It was 1966 all over again, because for one Ferrari driver, it was personal. The number 82 Ferrari 488, a privateer car supported by Houston-based Risi Competizione, was giving Richard Westbrook in the leading number 69 Ford GT all he could handle. At the wheel for Risi was Giancarlo Fisichella. No slouch on the Circuit de la Sarthe, Fisichella had two previous wins in this class, in 2012 and 2014, for the AF Corse team, which was also running Ferrari 488s this year. But the forty-three-year-old Italian was also a Formula One veteran, so he was one of motorsport's elites. For him, there was pride on the line.

And at 5:30, the weather was finally cooperating. The afternoon sun was out, the temperature had gone up, and it had become a lovely, breezy day for racing. The track was drying out, and the tires were heating up. The lap times were going down, and in GTE Pro, it was getting tight. It was Ford versus Ferrari, with the Corvettes and Porsches out of the lead action. The Porsches had been OK in the rain, but when the roads dried out, they simply couldn't find any speed, and the Corvettes' velocity hadn't shown up yet, despite the BOP tweaks to their restrictor plates.

With the summer solstice just a few days away, it was hours until nightfall, so the drivers got in some hard racing before the teams settled in to battle the darkness. And they raced hard: the Risi Competizione and AF Corse Ferraris took it to the GTs, moving into second and third positions, keeping the number 69 car fighting to hold its lead, while relegating the number 68 car to fourth.

But that lineup didn't last. The AF Corse Ferrari had to pit, with a mechanical problem, and the number 82 Risi 488 surged into the lead. Le Mans was a dogfight between the Blue Oval and the Prancing Stallion—and at this relatively early juncture, before the sun had set, it was clear that both carmakers had built machines with enough speed to keep matters lively. No lead would be safe for long.

It wasn't lost on anyone that the extremely impressive Ford Performance–Chip Ganassi Racing factory team with four cars was locked in a high-velocity duel with a pair of privateer teams wearing Ferrari red. The AF Corse team had been a Le Mans stalwart for years; Amato Ferrari (of no relationship to the car family) had launched AF in the mid-1990s, after retiring from a moderately successful racing career. Risi Competizione was the brainchild of

Giuseppe Risi, who started his team about the same time as AF Corse took off and has been connected with Ferrari ever since. The privateer teams don't have the same level of funding as the factory teams, but because Ferrari hasn't run a factory effort at Le Mans in decades, the privateers are the company's proxy. For Risi, both Fisichella and his fellow driver Toni Vilander hold the top driver classification, Platinum, and the team itself is well financed.

Nevertheless, it seemed as if a couple of Italian pirates were trying to spoil the party of America's second-largest automaker, as it fought to revisit what has gone down in history as the greatest humiliation Ferrari had ever experienced on a racetrack. At Ferrari, less successful road cars could be forgotten. But the loss at Le Mans in 1966 has never gone away. At Ferrari, existence begins and ends with racing. You may dream your entire life of owning a Ferrari, and you may become successful enough to buy one. But only a select few ascend the pantheon of speed that compelled Enzo Ferrari to build and sell cars to the public in the first place. Those people are the real drivers.

Even though the Ferrari factory abandoned Le Mans in the 1960s, the company's sports cars were always good enough on the track to continue with endurance racing, through the privateer teams. Giuseppe Risi was outspoken on this topic—he felt that it was the private teams that sustained sports-car racing when the big car companies shifted their focus. Without him and Amato Ferrari, there might have been no opportunity for Ford to stage its Le Mans comeback in 2016. Without them, Le Mans might have faded away.

And as the opening stage of the 2016 race drew to a close, Giuseppe Risi's number 82 Ferrari 488 was leading Le Mans. But the Ford teams weren't going to just sit back and take it.

"Our strategy was to win from the lead," Joey Hand told me later.

And why not? If you have four of the fastest cars, why fool around with late passes? Le Mans is an endurance race, and perhaps the biggest part of enduring its twenty-four hours, in the modern incarnation of the event, is to deliver monumental speed for a day and a night and another day. Ford's message was blunt: outrun us if you can. And only the Ferraris appeared capable of doing that.

There were two of them taking it to Ford. But even with a car off the lead lap, Ford still had a one-car advantage. If one of the Ferraris slipped back, it would be like a fox in the midst of a wolf pack, running for its life. So that was what it was all about—and what it would all be about, as one Ferrari and three Fords hurtled toward dusk.

Over the early evening, the Risi Ferrari opened up a lead, but Hand, in the number 68 GT, ran it down and took the lead. Then, at about 7:40 p.m., Ryan Briscoe's number 69 GT slipped past the number 82 Ferrari on the Mulsanne to take second place. Hand was still running first. So it was now Ford, Ford, Ferrari, one, two, three. The number 66 Ford was in fourth, while the number 67 car lagged after a return to the pits several hours back for additional repairs. The dry racing was clearly helping the quick cars. The Corvettes were struggling, and Porsche had fallen far back and lost a car to the garage. Aston Martin was intermittently in the mix. But this was a race for turbocharged supercars making 600 horsepower. The big V-8s were a sideshow.

A magical moment occurred at eight o'clock. Three Ford GTs were once again running one-two-three at the 24 Hours of Le Mans. But there were nineteen hours of racing to go, as the sun began very slowly setting over the usually quiet French countryside, now vibrating with the stupendous roar of high-revving engines. Back in Dearborn, they were starting to believe.

Before the race started, it wasn't entirely evident that they did, although the man at the top was setting a good example. About two hours into the race, I had ducked out of the media center and headed back down to the Ford paddock unit.

Mark Fields was hanging out with Bill Ford, both men outfitted in Ford Performance–branded gear and looking remarkably relaxed, a contrast to the edge I'd experienced with Nair and Pericak the day before. But everyone at Ford had a job to do. And the job of Fields and Bill Ford was to keep it chill, confident in the racing effort, while duly noting that they had committed an enormous sum of money to repeating history. I had asked around about how much and was told that I wouldn't believe if it I were told the truth. Or those I asked simply made something up. But running a single car for an endurance-racing season can cost between $1 million and $5 million, depending on the racing class, and those teams aren't building their cars from scratch. A run-of-the-mill new vehicle can cost a carmaker $1 billion to develop, so the actual racing aspect of the Ford return to Le Mans might have been the cheapest part of the whole deal (drivers might make only $25,000 for winning a race).

Fields immediately reminded me that Le Mans was the culmination of a process that Ford had set into motion when it had unveiled the new GT in January 2015. He had come to Le Mans later that year to announce the IMSA/WEC effort, but he hadn't been able to attend the Daytona debut for Ford Chip Ganassi Racing at the Rolex 24, owing to a conflict with a classic-car auction in Arizona, for which Ford was a major sponsor, bringing along a vehicle to be auctioned for charity.

"Raj and I had a deal," Fields said. "He'd go to Daytona, and I'd go to Barrett-Jackson."

Fields missed attending the disastrous debut in person—and although it probably wasn't his greatest test in leadership at Ford, it was still a test.

"Raj and I were texting back and forth, and he texted me the results. Then we talked, and we agreed that this is part of racing. If we, as a senior team, went back to the racing team and chewed their butts out, said, 'Goddammit, why did this happen?' we wouldn't have gotten the passion and motivation we need to be a winner."

Fields is one of those guys who never stop smiling, but it never seems smarmy, or as if he's trying to fool you into believing he's sincere. He's also always thinking, but not in a forced diplomatic way, to make sure he's on message. He was a tough guy from New Jersey who went to Harvard Business School after Rutgers and thrived at Ford because he was smart. He's not investment-banker or management-consultant smart, not that vicious kind of smart; he's warm smart.

"I came to Ford because of the people," he said. "Because of the community."

In Detroit, Fields proved over time that he cared deeply about the company and about what cars mean to those who adore them passionately—even though he freely admits that he isn't a "car guy," that he isn't a Bob Lutz or Lee Iacocca or really even a Mark Reuss.

"I don't have grease in my veins, but I love cars and trucks," he said.

That's a good thing, because Fields, an intense person who has learned how to employ his soft side with exactly the right amount of charisma, has a deep, emotional understanding of how to manage the ups and downs of other intense people.

He knew that Nair and Pericak were freaking out after Daytona. And he knew that Pericak in particular would beat himself senseless over the GT's messy coming-out party. And so he did what he always does now when confronted with a crisis, large or small, relevant to Ford's core business, Ford's future, or a Ford undertaking that is fraught with risk and unknowns—such as returning to the 24 Hours of Le Mans after a nearly five-decade absence.

"I've always run to the fire, taken the difficult assignments," he said.

But running to the fire in this instance was only part of what Fields did. He also channeled Alan Mulally. "'You went to Harvard Business School,'" they would say to me. "'You must have wanted to be CEO of Ford all along.' No, I just wanted to be the marketing manager for the Ford division."

Now he was CEO, but he wasn't going to be a demanding jerk. Fields was going to be a business guy who understood what makes an engineer's heart beat in his chest, and what makes an engineer's blood boil, and what would make an engineer lose sleep and yell at his kids. And he wasn't going to let those guys suffer alone. He was going to do what Mulally had taught him: he was going to empower them to see problems clearly and move rapidly to solve them.

After Daytona, you could tell that Pericak got it. I imagined the fall-on-my-sword moment with Nair and Fields. But the Ford CEO wasn't going to go there. As Nair had said before Daytona, things had been going too well. There is no glory without struggle.

"It's part of racing," Fields continued, as the roar of engines shot across the hundred yards of weathered French concrete that separated the Ford paddock unit from the stands. "You do the analysis. You say here's what went wrong and here's how we fix it. And you make sure you improve for the next race."

It was Mulally in a nutshell. The charts on the GT race cars had all been green. And then—*Boom!* A gigantic block of red. Fields was seasoned when it came to crisis. He embraced the trouble and saw it as a chance to bring the team together. If Pericak, Nair, Ganassi, and Larry Holt at Multimatic could get through this, the Le Mans assault would be stronger.

While we talked, Fields's choice was playing out in real time. And Ford was winning.

Everything was green now. Even the balky number 67 car had a chance to get back into it.

I like Mark Fields and I always have liked him. He's living proof that by reinventing your expectations, you can put yourself in a position to be great. Ford Performance and Ganassi needed Fields's effortless yet hard-won self-confidence and affirmation back in January, because at that point, the only people who really grasped that racing is hard and unpredictable were the drivers.

Even Chip Ganassi seemed to think that the Le Mans campaign wasn't starting out the way he thought it should—but for him it was more of a chain-of-command thing, and Chip Ganassi wasn't clearly at the very top.

"What I was most nervous about going into Daytona—and my nightmares came true—is that it was an adjustment for me and my team to be involved with a program with so many people touching the car that don't come under my direct command," Ganassi told me at Le Mans. "That was a challenge, a learning curve there. That was the tallest order of the spring, but it's behind us."

Ganassi also wasn't looking beyond Le Mans. "We're fully focused," he said. "We're here to win the race. I'm not planning next year. We're here to win this race this weekend."

He admitted that post–Le Mans, win or lose, the season would then revert to the mundane process of running races, weekend after weekend. "As big as those other races are, this is the one you want to win."

For me, that crystallized what the impending twenty-four-hour ordeal meant not just for Ganassi but for everyone at Ford. It was easy to argue that the GTs existed as new cars in a racing season, and that somehow it would be acceptable for them to in fact repeat the history of the GT40s and spend two years failing to win Le Mans while all the kinks were worked out.

"Everybody," Ganassi said, "wants to win the big ones."

He added, "The most competitive games attract the most competitive teams. It's an honor to be here. But you've still got to do the obvious things right. Take the tires off, put the tires on. Put the fuel in. Don't hit anybody. You've still got to the run the race. Even with all the fanfare and hoopla. You still have to just race. We're all in the middle of a chess game, and at three o'clock on Sunday at Le Mans, somebody is going to say 'checkmate.'"

Fields was in a similar state of mind. Before Saturday, June 18, 2016, I'd never seen an American CEO so fully and contentedly ensconced in the process of winning. But we talked for half an hour, about two hours into the race, and he never once looked up at the standings, which were displayed around the paddock unit on flat-screen monitors, constantly updated. He was along for the ride and glad to be a passenger. It was Pericak who was out in the trenches, in his racing suit and with the headset on, obsessing. And Fields knew Dave could handle the stress.

"I hope we win," Fields said, as we were shaking hands before I headed back to catch up on the race. "But if we don't, we'll learn some things."

Then he brought it right home: "And we'll be back next year."

I had been steadfast in my objectivity about Ford's chances since I had started following this story, back in mid-2015, when the company confirmed that it would return to Le Mans. What I really wanted was competition, drama, six months of adventures and misadventures on and off the track. You know, a good story.

But I had to admit it, as I walked back to the stands: I wanted Ford to win. The symbolism was just too rich, too heady. In 2009, the American auto industry had been down, out, and looking as though it might not get back up again. Ford had been in better shape than GM and Chrysler but not in *great* shape. It had been, as Fields had put it, "harrowing." And yet we were all, seven years later, coming off the best sales year in the history of the U.S. auto market—17.5 million new cars and trucks had rolled off dealer lots—and Ford was back at Le Mans with a true factory effort for the first time since 2010 (privateers had run the second-generation GT back then). Heck, General Motors was here, as well, with the Corvette Racing team.

I was having my own "America! Fuck, yeah!" moment. I was thinking about getting a tattoo of the Circuit de la Sarthe on my forearm before I left France.

But I didn't want Ferrari to throw in the towel, and as night arrived and the race moved into a period when the nerves start to fray, the adrenaline begins to ebb, the drivers try but fail to sleep, and the cars begin to feel and show the deleterious effects of lap after lap after lap, Ferrari lived up to its legendary status as the greatest racing marque to ever turn a wheel in competition.

With midnight closing in and sunrise six hours away, with a nearly full moon casting white light across the blissfully dry Circuit de la Sarthe, it was Ford-Ford-Ferrari-Ford on the lead lap. Only the number 82 Risi 488 stood between Ford and a full repeat of the 1966 result. But that Ferrari 488 was one hell of a car. And as night passed, dawn arrived, and pursuit of glory in France continued into Sunday afternoon, we'd learn that Giancarlo Fisichella is one hell of a driver.

Chapter 14

Fifty Years to the Day

Attrition always becomes a factor on the Circuit de la Sarthe. In 2016, in the prototype classes, cars were on and off the track, in and out of the garage, all night long. I devoted only one eye to the class that would ultimately claim the Le Mans title outright, but Toyota seemed impressive. I noted that no Japanese manufacturer had won Le Mans since Mazda in 1991.

The Michelin lounge had a convenient view straight down into the Ford pits, so I meandered over for a snack and to see whether the Ganassi crews could get their drivers in and out quickly and cleanly in the darkness.

The food had been delightful for the whole of my time at Le Mans. At races in the United States, I was used to urns of stale coffee, soda machines, maybe some bland sandwiches rolled out for lunch. The only deviation since I had dived into both the car-show circuit and the sports-car racing season in January had been a cocktail party thrown by an organization of journalists I belong to, the International Motor Press Association, at the conclusion of the New York auto show in April.

In France there were sandwiches, but they were made of mouth-watering French ham and tasty cheese and they were delicately sliced into narrow rectangles. There were other cheeses and fruits. Young men and women in black suits, white shirts, and black neckties would happily pour you a Coke or a beer or a glass of wine or some Champagne. There was espresso or cappuccino on demand. At one point, two chefs arrived to prepare elaborate little haute cuisine concoctions that could be nibbled from small cups. If you wanted to, you could grab a copy of the red Michelin Guide to take home; there were about 100 neatly arranged on a bank of shelves.

Overall, though, Le Mans was frankly looking a bit shabby. The press facilities appeared as if they hadn't been significantly updated since the 1970s. The worn concrete stands did not mimic those in the shiny speed palaces of America. But this was still France—food mattered.

As it turned out, the timing of my snack was serendipitous, because the number 66 GT was sitting in the pits. It sat motionless for much longer than would have been normal for a refueling or a tire change, especially for a car that was fighting to hold onto third place in the GTE Pro class. At Le Mans, tire changes and refills can't happen simultaneously, and the engines have to be turned off when fuel is taken on. Teams warm new tires up in special ovens beforehand, so they hit the cars hot and are ready to rock without a warm-up lap, a boon at night when the temperatures fall. But something unrelated to tires and fuel was keeping the number 66 at bay.

The problem was a malfunction with the electronics that should have kept the green "66" on its flank illuminated. Unable to identify the car, the marshals had ordered it into the pits, where crew members in racing suits, helmets, and gloves had frantically disassembled and were reassembling the components.

It was a serious infraction to have any aspect of the lighting system fail at night. This was an endurance race, and a healthy chunk of it, some eight hours, was run in darkness. A car that didn't have reliable lights was obviously failing a critical test.

I'd later find out that the 66 wasn't the only GT experiencing electronics issues. But it was the only one of the three on the lead lap that would get knocked off because of them.

The fix on the 66 car was fiddly and time-consuming. The crewman who was completing the repair was dealing with tiny screws smaller than pushpins and a precise, narrow screwdriver in the middle of the night, with a helmet on. The pits are well lit at Le Mans, but it was still a comically delicate crisis to be suffering through. From where I watched, the crewman was doing a brilliant job. He didn't drop a single screw.

I later learned that this episode was classic Le Mans. A glitch that no one had planned for showed up in the middle of the night. The fix had to be figured out fast, and a solution had to be improvised. And then a mechanic or crew member had to execute it, under the most glaring pressure imaginable.

After about ten minutes, the problem was finally corrected, and the GT roared off into the night. But now it was two Fords versus one Ferrari on the lead lap.

Ferrari seized its chance to lead the GTE Pro class before twelve hours of racing had been completed. The number 68 Ford came into the pits for a brake change—something that had to be done at some point during the twenty-four hours of racing—dropping well behind the number 82 Risi 488, which went on to open a sizable time gap. The number 69 GT moved into second place, but it had its own brake change to deal with at some point.

Overnight, the Fords chased the Ferrari, while elsewhere in GTE Pro, the AF Corse Ferrari 488 crashed and later retired from the race, and one of the two Porsche 911s running in the class blew an engine. These mishaps and incidents—along with those in the other classes—might have brought out the safety car in previous years, but Le Mans now employs slow zones, requiring cars to reduce speed in affected parts of the circuit, dipping to fifty miles per hour when there's an accident or a problem on the circuit. The race marshals monitor progress through these areas, and the circuit itself is equipped with a signal system to alert the drivers to slow down or suffer a penalty. (One of the secret skills in winning Le Mans is remaining constantly aware of the rules, so that a minor infraction doesn't undo hours of work.) The implementation of the slow zone keeps the race moving, but it makes catching up with a fast car from a deficit of even a single lap difficult, because you can't run flat out.

The Risi Ferrari fought hard, but the Fords were able to stay in touch, and by sunrise, the number 68 GT had closed the gap and was in the Ferrari's mirrors. Then disaster struck: the charging Ford was assessed a drive-through penalty for failing to shut off its engine during refueling in the pits; it would have to make a slow detour through pit lane, entering, then exiting, without stopping, losing a bit of time. The number 69 GT might be Ford's only hope, but it would have to make up ground on the Risi Ferrari.

Sunrise also brought carnage, as the return of daylight sent a signal through the prototype class to get on it and go for the black-and-white flag. For the GTE Pro drivers, this was a risky patch, where they had the potential to get involved in crashes as the faster prototypes start to fight it out. For the lead Ferrari and the Fords, however, nothing bad happened. And the Fords started to use their speed.

The pass came, naturally, on the Mulsanne Straight, with Joey Hand in the number 68 car, which had stormed back from its penalty. The American slipped around the Italian driver Matteo Malucelli and stepped on it hard to get in front of the 488. Hand wasn't in the simulator in North Carolina. This was reality, on the most famous racing stretch on planet Earth.

We're going to win from the lead.

Four hours to go, and Ford was once again running first in its class. An hour later, and it was still Ford-Ferrari, one-two. The 69 and 66 GTs were third and fourth.

But it was snug at the top. Hand had to keep the Ferrari back. And it was rough in that Ferrari. Toni Vilander, a thirty-five-year-old from Finland with two Le Mans wins with AF Corse to his credit, had to hold the number 68 Ford in his sights while making sure that the number 69 GT didn't start pressuring him from behind.

The phrase "Go like hell" is ingrained in Le Mans lore. It's what Bruce McLaren shouted to Chris Amon during a driver change in 1966. It's a rallying cry. But I've always thought that the phrase, for all its urgent simplicity, cuts both ways. Going like hell is all about balls-to-the-wall driving and doing the most basic thing it takes to win, go faster than the other guy. But hell is, of course, what it has always been: a place of eternal suffering, a lake of fire, the realm of satanic ordeal, a region where you abandon all hope. Hell isn't a place you want to get too familiar with. And going like hell in a race car is a mind-set that you want to visit only at the right time and in the right place.

Hell was more than a state of mind in the Risi Competizione Ferrari 488, blasting down the Mulsanne Straight at 200 miles per hour, its whistling twin turbos and screaming 606-horsepower V-8 filling Vilander's ears with mechanical anguish, while on the radio he received updates about the Ford in front of him and the Fords behind. Now was the time to press, in the competitive conflagration that his body and mind had become, locked in a bright red missile that had been racking up eight-mile laps at an average speed of 150 miles per hour for almost twenty hours.

Predictably, it was in the so-called Porsche Curves on the opposite side of the circuit from the Mulsanne that the Ferrari lost it. Right. Left. More left. Right again. It's a critical section. You *have to* be quick here. You want to push for the fastest line, but that might cause you to deviate from the racing line, the black track of sticky rubber laid down over the course of hundreds of laps by dozens of cars. It helps you stay glued to the surface and it gives you a guide though the curves, like a worn footpath when you're in an unfamiliar forest.

But just off the racing line, the surface can be treacherous. The car can slip if the power is being laid down and the bond between rubber and road isn't quite right. And when you're trying to win Le Mans, you can't back off on the power unless you're sitting on a big fat lead. You can't lose speed. It's the *can't* that creates the danger.

You can relax on the Mulsanne Straight, sort of. It's your right foot and the car. Keep it pointed straight. You're a passenger. You can get on the radio and talk to the team. But you're a driver in the Porsche Curves.

Vilander was getting the 68 GT lined up. Another lap maybe. Another run down the Mulsanne. But he couldn't lose *anything* in the Porsche Curves. He knew the number 68 Ford was fast—it had already run the Ferrari drivers down when it looked as if they had stretched out a lead. Now he was doing the running down. But he and Risi didn't have eight hours of racing to work with. They had three. And the Porsche Curves were his undoing.

"I tried to catch Joey," he said later. "But I overestimated my skills."

Vilander's car went into a spin. It wasn't wrecked—his talent kept the car in the race—but Risi's shot at spoiling Ford's win had ended. The number 68 GT's lead of less than ten seconds would grow to forty with two and a half hours to go. The commentators on the TV broadcast say they don't think the number 82 Ferrari can get it back. But the race was far from a done deal.

The number 68 GT, now with Dirk Müller at the wheel, was running fast in the front. But the car was beset with electronics problems and had been all night. Nothing cost it a disastrous amount of time (the same couldn't be said of the number 66 Ford), but at various points when Sébastien Bourdais was driving, he hadn't had a working radio, and he didn't have good control over the car.

Bourdais had been trying to win Le Mans flying blind and driving by feel, with no updates from mission control back in the pits on a track that is eight miles long and takes almost four minutes to get around. He didn't know how much gas he actually had. He didn't know how fast he was going coming into the pits. So he couldn't comply with the Le Mans rules, which strictly and precisely govern how cars enter and leave the pits, and the sequence by which fuel goes in, tires come on and off, and other legal pit maintenance can go down.

It had been a steering-wheel problem that was responsible for the pit-lane drive-through penalty. When the fuel was going in while the driver change was under way, Bourdais simply couldn't shut the car off using the switch on the steering wheel, and as a result, Ford got busted. The glitches hadn't returned after the team put a new steering wheel on the number 68 car, so the nervous task at hand for Müller was to stay cool but stay fast. Müller had Fisichella thirty-six seconds behind him. John Hindhaugh, the English broadcaster who had jumped onto the TV feed for the conclusion of the race, boomed out the obvious.

"Giancarlo Fisichella is surrounded by the remaining Ford GTs!"

He *was* surrounded. It was a lonely struggle. But in the Risi number 82 Ferrari, Fisichella wasn't giving up. He was giving all.

Fisichella was an Italian race-car driver with two Le Mans wins in his trophy case, not to mention an impressive Formula One career. He had been behind the wheel for as long he could remember.

If one of his three children asks him what Papà does for a living, he might answer that he takes a machine built for speed and uses his talent to make that speed into something that wins races. Now he was at the wheel of the fastest Ferrari sports car he'd ever driven. It wasn't F1-car fast. But it was fast. And he was doing what anyone who races Ferraris was made to do, what he was made to do. He was bonded with his 488. He felt the Circuit de la Sarthe fly by just inches below his seat. He felt his tires and the horsepower of his engine, and he heard the high-pitched whistle of its twin turbos at full song. There was no fighting the car, only flow. And he wasn't going to go down without fighting the Fords.

But honestly, objectively, was Fisichella going to catch Müller in the number 68 GT? Probably not. It was the pole car. It was fast—faster than the number 82 Ferrari 488. But speed isn't everything. Maybe the moment would get to Müller. The guy is forty. He had never won Le Mans before. He took a third in 2011, but that was five years ago. You can lose a lot in five years. He had to handle the Porsche Curves, too. *He had to win from the lead.*

Fisichella also had to think about the number 69 GT on his tail. Running second sucks. It's almost like running two races at the same time. Fisichella had to try to win, with everything he had left, and avoid finishing third—or worse, *fourth.* You can see the contradiction. By pressing for first, Vilander had stumbled and spun the car. Was Fisichella good enough to avoid a stumble—and to win?

The answer was no. "We just didn't have enough speed," he would say later. In the end, that's what it came down to.

As a crowd of the Ford faithful—many of them students of the 1966 win, some of them owners of the mid-2000s GT—waved blue Ford flags and hooted and hollered from the balcony of the Ford hospitality tent overlooking the appropriately named Ford Chicanes, which the cars negotiate as they power back past the stands and the pits, Dirk Müller got the job done, without cracking.

"The last few laps were very emotional," he would say after the race.

Fisichella got his second. "We deserved it," he said, unsmiling, when he got out of the car.

The number 69 GT driven by Ryan Briscoe, Richard Westbrook, and Scott Dixon completed the Ford-Ferrari-Ford, one-two-three finish for 2016. It was *almost* 1966 all over again. And it had been Ford versus Ferrari. There was certainly some poetry in that, to me, anyway—and to Dave Pericak. "You couldn't have scripted it any better," he later said to me.

The Risi Ferrari drivers, however, were grim and miserable, even later. But that was appropriate. They had fought a gallant fight, and their consolation was justified unhappiness. No one would begrudge them being crestfallen after losing such a bold campaign. It hurts when you could win and you don't, regardless of the history. It hurts for a long time.

"They deserved second place," Dave Pericak told me. "I never thought for one moment that Ferrari wasn't going to give us a fight. But I would have loved to see a Ford in second."

Ford had initially considered a post-race complaint against the number 82 Ferrari. Its leader lights had malfunctioned after the sun came up, the same problem that the number 66 GT had dealt with at night. But, showing commendable sportsmanship, Ford never made the complaint official.

The number 66 Ford GT of Olivier Pla, Stefan Mücke, and Billy Johnson took fourth. For Mücke in particular it was wonderful vindication after his harrowing crash just a month earlier at Spa. The number 67 car, driven by Marino Franchitti, Andy Priaulx, and Harry Tincknell, was never a factor and finished ninth in the GTE Pro class and fortieth overall. It had never overcome the lap deficit it racked up owing to the broken gearbox at the start of the race, but it did finish.

The GTs were grimy and battle scarred, with bits of cracked carbon fiber and duct tape spoiling their smooth shells. They were splattered with black, like sinewy supermodels that had spent twenty-four hours drilling for oil. But no one had ever been more interested in studying their curves and angles. They glowed from within.

It was a new victory for Ford, a stunning achievement, fresh history, and a majestic comeback from the debacle at Daytona. The horrible start in January had been vindicated by an ultimately magical return to France in June.

But it wasn't the only big story to come out of Le Mans in 2016. In fact, it was overshadowed by what befell the Toyota LMP1-H prototype car.

The number 5 Toyota had a lead of almost seventy seconds over the number 2 Porsche, running away with the race. But with twenty-three hours and fifty-five minutes of racing completed, the Toyota lost power. It stalled completely, in front of the stands, and the Porsche went past. One more lap, and Porsche repeated 2015, the overall winner of Le Mans.

The Toyota team was devastated; it would have been the first win by a Japanese team in twenty-five years. Instead, it was the most unbelievable finish in the history of the 24 Hours of Le Mans, a meltdown on the cusp of victory that will likely never be forgotten, even if Toyota wins this thing ten times in a row.

Because you're involved in the same race, just running it in less outlandish cars, you feel for Toyota if you're a Ford driver, or if you're Chip Ganassi, or if you're Raj Nair or Dave Pericak or Henry Ford III or Bill Ford or anyone else in the Ford family who touched the incredible story of the new GT and its return to glory at the toughest race in the world. You don't want to see another strong, factory-supported effort done in at the last possible moment by a bizarre mechanical fault. But you're also entitled to your victory lap and your podium celebration. A win is a win, no matter what else happens on the track.

Bill Ford joined the drivers on the podium for the trophy presentation and the ritual spraying of Champagne from gigantic bottles—bottles that the drivers wouldn't surrender, continuing to chug the bubbly as they were led to the cramped Le Mans pressrooms for post-race questions. The "Star-Spangled Banner" was playing, echoing across the French countryside, a quiet place once again, as the cacophony of racing engines had vanished.

The race was in the record books. The drivers gathered in the pressroom and talked informally about how tired they were. I asked Joey Hand where Dirk Müller was, and Hand said that he had gone to get his phone. They were all on their phones. There was exciting news to convey to friends and family.

"Let me ask you a serious question," I said to Hand.

"I didn't get my sausage Egg McMuffin," he said, preempting me with what had become an inside joke.

He was dead-dog beat, you could tell. Hand is a compulsively cheerful person, but he was digging deep. The buzz hadn't worn off. He was looking forward to getting back to see his kids. They had been learning to play golf. There was a vacation planned. But there were also more races to run.

"That's not a serious question!" I countered.

There was a McDonald's just off the Mulsanne Straight, but Hand hadn't been able to make it over there before race time, he told me with a mischievous smile. But he had managed to cobble together a facsimile from what he could find in the morning, an improvised McDonald's good-luck charm far, far from home, an impromptu *McMuffin avec saucisson*.

Then I asked the serious question, taking him back to his lead in the Daytona race before all the problems showed up with his car. What was it like to run in front there in the GT's debut, only to see it all go wrong, and then today take the lead over Ferrari when Malucelli was at the wheel?

He thanked me for remembering his briefly impressive driving debut with the GT, then rose wearily to his feet and got ready to do for Ford what he was paid to do—after doing what he had just done in such an effective way that he could now claim kinship with McLaren and Amon and the racing brotherhood of 1966.

"My father always told me," Hand said to me, clearly fighting his exhaustion, "if you can pass 'em, do it."

Ford wasn't always winning the 24 Hours of Le Mans in 2016. But its cars were winning the race for longer than any others in their class. And the number 68 car had won the pole, and although it hadn't led the entire race, it finished where it started.

"Very few races have the passion and substance that this one does," Scott Dixon, the first New Zealander to win the Indy 500 (in 2008), said during the post-race press conference.

Dixon was a lot like Fisichella, the Formula One guy now racing sports cars—but Dixon had *won* the Indy 500. Fisichella had been a Formula One winner, but he'd never captured an F1 championship. You got the sense that Le Mans was something special for Dixon.

"I love it," he said. He had finished third, but it didn't seem that way. "It's fantastic," he added.

One difficult thing about a car race is that it ends, even the longest and most challenging one. I was familiar with the feeling, the ebbing of the rush. Le Mans was a mess. In one spot, I noticed at least two dozen empty beer cans. The carnival was being disassembled, the Ferris wheel was coming down, the booze had run dry, the colorful tents were disappearing, the crêpes were running out. The revelers were packing up to go home, and the parking lots were emptying.

But I took a minute to soak it all in anyway. Racing, when you get right down to it, is about the *sound* as much as anything. It's music. Those engines, they grab you in the gut. It's a sacred sound, a siren cry, a raw and cruel symphony. Men have died for it. Fifty years ago to the day, the GT40s had crossed the finish line one-two-three. On June 19, 2016, the GT had almost matched that performance: one-three-four.

A racetrack is never completely silent. The motors echo across the generations. I closed my eyes and opened my ears. I listened for the old sounds to combine with the new.

Epilogue

I was standing on pit lane at Lime Rock Park in Lakeville, Connecticut, talking to Joey Hand for the first time since Le Mans. It was about an hour before the start of the IMSA WeatherTech Northeast Grand Prix, at a tight little track that was built in 1957 and became famous when a local racing enthusiast named Paul Newman decided it was going to be his stomping ground. There was, it turned out, a McDonald's in nearby Canaan. Mission accomplished.

Hand had followed up the Le Mans victory with a second-place finish at Sahlen's Six Hours of the Glen, at Watkins Glen International in New York's Finger Lakes region. Westbrook and Briscoe took home the win, making it a one-two sweep for Ford-Ganassi. The program was back to running two cars per race for the rest of the season in the United States and Europe. Hand was on an impressive run, as was Ford.

It was a beautiful day in Connecticut for the grand prix, the pale blue northeastern summer sky filled with enormous clouds, the surrounding hills a deep and lush green. But it was *hot*—and the temperature was going to climb to well over 100 degrees inside the number 66 that Hand would be piloting around the bucolic, unpretentious, but treacherously snug Lime Rock course. That didn't stop him from doing a little dance, a back-and-forth shuffle, when I asked him what it felt like to be a Le Mans winner.

"That makes everything OK," he said, with his signature grin.

Ford didn't win at Lime Rock, but Westbrook and Briscoe took third in a wild race that saw Fisichella run off the track twice during the two-hour-and-forty-minute dash. For me, the story had come almost full circle. As at Daytona, Corvette Racing finished one-two, the team that had been completely out of it at Le Mans capturing its hundredth win.

There was something soothing about the relatively quiet environs of Lime Rock and its small-town vibe after the speed palace in Florida and the Colosseum of endurance racing in France, and Hand seemed almost serene.

"It's been a busy season," he said. Right after the Lime Rock race, he would head off for a short vacation before getting back to it at the ten-hour Petit Le Mans race at Road Atlanta in September.

On the other side of the concrete pit barrier, on pit lane itself, two GTs were parked at forty-five-degree angles, the cockpits covered with silvery insulating blankets to keep the interiors cool for race time. They looked fresh and clean and ready to rock, just as they had on the grid at Daytona seven months earlier. Now, of course, they were Le Mans winners. The new GT had supplanted the old GT40. Ford had crafted a new legend.

Dave Pericak was a changed man when I finally caught up with him. He missed Lime Rock because he had to head to Germany for the 6 Hours of Nürburgring the same weekend, but he was still enjoying the post–Le Mans buzz. You had to hand it to the guy: In January, he had declared that Ford was ready to race, only to run smack into the catastrophe at Daytona. But now that bad memory had been erased by the most spectacular achievement of his already pretty stellar career with Ford.

"We took the trophy back to Dearborn and had a celebration," he recalled, after saying that he began to calm down and appreciate the Le Mans win only on the plane back to the United States. "Something like four thousand people turned out, when it was over ninety degrees."

Everyone at Ford had been following Pericak's every move, listening to his every utterance, sharing in the ups and downs, the wins and losses. And although his emotions had been a challenge to manage throughout the year, Pericak's confidence in the GT and the racing team, and in Multimatic and Ford itself, never waned.

"I knew we could do it," he said. "To see Joey make that pass, to do it on command, that proved there was no looking back. I really felt that if the car stayed together, we had it won. Winning Le Mans had a way of washing away a lot of the pain and fears that had emerged early in the season."

After the balance-of-performance controversy in France, he was also glad Ford had followed up Le Mans immediately with the Watkins Glen one-two victory. "That made a statement and closed the book on the skepticism."

Pericak was optimistic about his future—and happy about his job, looking forward to finishing up the IMSA/WEC season and going for a championship. He'd be back for the 2017 Le Mans campaign as well. "If they don't fire me, I'm planning to stick around."

On July 28, Mark Fields presented Ford's second-quarter 2016 earnings, the company's first report after Le Mans, to Wall Street. Fields was only the second Ford top boss, and the first whose name wasn't on the Glass House, to win the race.

Ford was continuing to make money, piling up profitable quarter after profitable quarter. Unless the economy was to get cratered by something totally out of Ford's control, the company coffers were adequately stocked to keep it going back to Le Mans for the rest of the decade. Would four consecutive wins in the late 1960s be matched or exceeded in the late 2010s? Everyone at Ford hoped so, and the company was ready to put its money behind its magnificent new Le Mans–conquering GT. But Ferrari, Porsche, and, most important, Corvette weren't going to sit out the next few years. History can't ever be perfectly replayed, of course. Ferrari wanted revenge. Corvette wanted redemption. The plot points were already in place for other carmakers to stage their own returns to glory.

When Lime Rock was over, I walked back to the parking lot and thought about why auto racing exerts such a powerful emotional pull on the human psyche. There's always something melancholy about the hours right after the end of a race, especially if the sun is slowly setting as the venue is cleaned up, the race cars are stowed in their semitruck transporters, and everyone who's part of motorsport's gypsy spectacle heads for the next contest. But this time does give you the opportunity to take a close look at the racetrack. I always check out the racing line, that black, grippy streak made from the bits of tires that burn off as the drivers sling through the corners and down the straights.

In a way the racing line is high-performance automotive artwork, the only tangible thing the machine leaves behind, like a signature that will rapidly fade. But just after the race, it tells a story. Something remarkable happened here. We made something incredible. We brought it here and pushed ourselves. We ached and burned. We went fast. We looked down the track and lived a few seconds in the future. We risked injury or even death. For two hours—or six or twelve or twenty-four—we could touch all the danger and excitement and promise that anyone in human history could ever ask for.

Acknowledgments

I'm grateful for the support, assistance, and inspiration of the many people who helped make this remarkable story happen. My agent, Dan Mandel, at Sanford J. Greenburger Associates, came up with the idea after a conversation with my stupendous, dapper editor, Grove Atlantic's Jamison Stoltz, and from there it was a wild ride for a year, taking me from Florida to France, with stops in Detroit, Los Angeles, and Paris.

At Ford, Bill Collins was the first person I told about the project, and he immediately put me in touch with Paul Seredynski, who then connected me with Dave Pericak and Ford Performance. Mark Fields was generous with his time, as was Henry Ford III. Alan Mulally declined to be interviewed more kindly than anyone else in my professional experience. Raj Nair was forthcoming at exactly the right time, while Ray Day made sure that I got the executive access I needed. Rhonda Belluso told me the first of many inspiring One Ford tales. Mary Beth Childs made my transition from West Coast to East Coast motoring journalist an easy one, and Whitney Eichinger introduced me to Bob Shanks, whose regular insights into the nuts and bolts of Ford's business were invaluable. In Europe, Marcus Baumann made life easy for me as I dealt with my first Le Mans. Francesca Montini set me up with Moray Callum, and Moray was his usual entertaining self on the top-secret design of the GT.

Amko Leenarts provided an additional point of view. Mike Levine kept me up-to-date on all things related to Ford trucks. At Lincoln, Kumar Galhotra, supported by David Woodhouse, provided me with a fantastic story line about renewal, while Amy Horta kept me in the loop with all the news. Special thanks as well to Warren Crone at Ford Images.

At General Motors, Mary Barra was a great interview, and Mark Reuss was never less than straightforward and candid about his ups and downs. Both helped expand the scale of my narrative. Thanks to David Albritton and Jordana Strosberg for their assistance with the executive suite at the Renaissance Center. Tony Cervone has been a fine guide to GM's post-bankruptcy transformation, and Tom Henderson provided me with terrific access to Chuck Stevens, who is as sharp as they come on the auto industry. Kimberly Carpenter represents Chevrolet very capably in the Northeast, and Steve Martin has kept me steadily posted as Cadillac becomes a New York auto brand. Johan de Nysschen helped explain Cadillac to me. Ray Wert has a terrific eye for what makes a good digital-media story, and the incomparable Pierre Kanter has been a true friend and confidant.

At IMSA, Nate Siebens ensured that I got what I needed from my visit to Daytona, and Scott Atherton gave me my first juicy indication that the GT had almost been a Mustang.

Elodie Leboulleux and Inge Moreau Horsten of Le Mans and the ACO were immensely helpful and ever gracious with media accreditation for the 24 Heures.

Coralie Garandeau and Olivier Mirguet and their sons, Achille and Raoul, were welcoming in Paris before Le Mans, and their hospitality, as well as their guesthouse, enabled me to complete a large part of the book before I left France.

At Ferrari, Morgan Theys, Didier Theys, Krista Florin, and Efrain Olivares started the journey to Le Mans with me at Daytona and ended it in France. Special thanks are due to Giancarlo Fisichella, as great a driver as has ever slipped behind the wheel.

Khobi Brooklyn and Alexis Georgeson at Tesla have helped with countless stories about their company, as has Elon Musk himself. Led Zeppelin provided the sound track for my writing, and I doubt I'll get another chance to thank Robert Plant, Jimmy Page, John Paul Jones, and the late John Bonham, so what the hell? Thanks, Zep!

Special thanks to Alistair Watkins and Sophie Stansfield of Influence Sports, whom I met at Daytona, and who saved my life in Le Mans, after I had been up all night and was more than ready for the Rolex-hosted media breakfast when the sun rose. Equal thanks to the Michelin Guide staff, who kept us all provisioned through the long night.

Many thanks to my colleagues at *Business Insider*, especially Benjamin Zhang, Will Fierman, Mo Hadi, Christina Sterbenz, Justin Gmoser, Hollis Johnson, Ashley Lutz, Julie Zeveloff, and our fearless founder, Henry Blodget. A special mention for Jim Ledbetter and Elinor Shields at *Slate*'s *The Big Money*, where I wrote about the Detroit meltdown every day for two years. And thanks to Madeleine Brand of KCRW, who occasionally lets me come on her radio show, *Press Play*, to talk cars.

My colleagues in the auto writing game are too numerous to mention with any comprehensiveness, but I'm grateful to all of them, collectively, for keeping this mad passion for writing about automobiles, both fast and slow, alive.

I owe a debt of gratitude to Chip Ganassi and his spectacular team of drivers, on both sides of the Atlantic. In particular, I'm grateful to Joey Hand for his always-cheerful embrace of competition, speed, and ultimately, victory.

Amy Hughes provided stupendous, scrupulous copyediting, Susan Gamer executed a careful and thorough proofread, and the production and design teams at Grove Atlantic, directed by Julia Berner-Tobin, created a gorgeous finished book. Special thanks to Nicole Nyhan for getting this book across the finish line. Will Pittenger created a marvelous map of the Circuit de la Sarthe, and George Gibson, Deb Seager, and Amy Hundley sent the book out into the world with great engagement and professionalism.

Finally, thanks and adoration go to my lovely and brilliant wife, Maria Russo, who helped me in countless ways all along. Our children—August Larkin, Mario James, and Dante Nicholas—never stopped asking me how the book was going. Pressure and motivation, all at the same time! In the end, it was a family effort, with even my mother, Nora, and my in-laws, Mario and Jacquie Russo, kicking in encouragement and enthusiasm.